My ValHalla

By

Celia LaVon Belt

ISBN-13 979-8-218-47393-8

Photography by John Mohar

Text layout and design by Watercress Press

Angels Are No Strangers To Chains

I dedicate this book to my father, Robert Winston VanBibber

Yours Always,

LaVon

Prologue

This book is filled with facts, and there is no fiction. Some of you may find it difficult to believe and perhaps disturbing to read. It is a full account of events that took place between October 4th, 2022, and March 2024. I have tried to recreate events, locales and conversations from my memories of them. I write this book not to "tell a story." I write to ease my pain and suffering. I also write in the hopes that my tough lessons on this earth inspire you and plant the seed to be good to others. Always remember that forgiveness is an act and a choice. For those of you who have read my first two books, you know I am no stranger to pain, suffering, and brutal treatment. I am a Survivor. It is what I do best, what I was chosen to do, and what I must continue to do.

Au commencement

I woke up early, 5 a.m. to be exact. I sat in blessed silence, clutching my favorite coffee cup and thinking sweet thoughts of Randy, my husband. He crossed over on December 23rd, 2017, and I never cease to remember our times together. We were hunting buddies, best friends, and lovers. Treasured memories flood my mind. Our marriage was not perfect, yet it was cast in the heavens. Our stars were always there, waiting for one another, as they will forever be.

Left:

Randy and I in Namibia, Africa

We fought like cats and dogs and loved like lions. I will never forget that man and the joy he brought into my life. He was my one true love. He was my moon, and I, his sun. Together, we were cast like stars. Seen only on the brightest of nights.

The birds were busy at their feeders, and my beloved hummingbirds were in abundance. The sun was already hot on my skin, producing a good sweat. The sound of the waterfall cascading into the pool was like balm to this soul of mine, and I took in the way the leaves moved in the breeze. They almost appeared to dance with one another to a secret tune only they could hear. After my coffee and a good read spent by the fire pit, I began my day as I did every day, watering the front lawn, trees, and plants. It was still brutally hot, one of the hottest summers on record for this part of Texas. I decided to change into some shorts before beginning work in the backyard. I stripped off my sweat-soaked tank and jeans, exchanging them for an old pair of cut-offs and a comfy t-shirt. That's as far as I got.

I barely had the cut-offs up and had not yet put on my t-shirt when it struck. A grand mal seizure. Something I had never experienced, and it was utterly terrifying. My body was shaking uncontrollably, my eyesight was diverting, and my mind was not my own. I was not in control, and I was desperate to seek some help. Since my riding accident in 2017, I have experienced many mini-mal seizures, which were kept under control with medications; I had been prescribed Keppra and Topiramate to control the seizure activity in three lobes of my brain. Living with a traumatic brain injury had become my norm. The seizures, vertigo, and confusion had become staples of my life. I was incredibly blessed to have my service dog, Taboo, constantly at my side. Not only could he detect seizures, but he also guided me at night, leading me safely to the bathroom and the kitchen for my water refills. In addition to Taboo, I had Risqué. Both were imported from the Czech Republic. They were both incredibly bright and intuitive. They offered a level of love and protection that you simply cannot put a value on. I loved them, and since losing Randy, they were a constant in my life; I loved them as if they were my children.

What could have caused such a seizure? I had decided to stop taking lorazepam; this drug was prescribed to me for seizures in the third lobe of my brain. I'd been taking it since 2017. My daughter had voiced on several occasions her fears that she felt this particular medication was taking its toll on me. I would simply pass out once I had ingested it. I tapered myself off this drug just eight days before I experienced this grand mal seizure. I had also recently begun working on my third book, *My Valhalla*. I found myself experiencing vivid memories of the burn unit. Flashbacks that I never care to remember.

Right –

My loves: Taboo and Risqué.

As a volunteer on the burn unit at Brooke Army Medical Center and the founder of The Moonlight Fund, I was constantly in the "heat," so to speak. I was either volunteering, working long hours to raise money for the fund, or caring for burn survivors' needs on a daily basis. The stress I experienced and the sights I took in during those days I buried somewhere deep down inside me. I began volunteering on the burn unit in 1998 and quickly thereafter co-founded Moonlight Fund, Inc. I was on the unit during the wars in Iraq and Afghanistan; I saw, smelled, and experienced things I would never speak of. Each day, as I laid my hand on that fourth floor door to the burn unit, a part of my brain turned off, disconnect as I entered that world, it was the only way to survive what I was about to encounter and as I exited each day, I would regroup, forget what I had just seen, heard and felt. Could it have been one, or perhaps a combination of both, that brought on such a serious seizure?

I knew I had to get to the front door. My painter, Armando, needed his pay, and I desperately needed medical attention. I flung open the front door, still in the throes of a full-blown seizure episode. I had no thought process, no idea that I stood half-dressed, breasts exposed, and body flailing about uncontrollably. Armando was still in the front yard by the grace of the Gods. Seeing me in such a state had to have been disturbing for him. E.M.S. was called to the scene. I have no memories other than that of a canine officer, arms extended, guiding my two German Shepherds, Taboo and Risqué, back into the house. I was later told that I was found seizing with my two dogs standing over me. They were there to protect and care for me. I can still see the canine police officer, arms outstretched, guiding my beloved two dogs back into the house. Other than that, I have no memories.

I remember nothing of the next eleven hours. When I woke up, I was strapped down by my ankles in a psychiatric unit. I continued to have grand mal seizures, unable to move my legs. The seizures lasted for what seemed like hours. One after another, there was nothing I could do but lie there and pray they would end. I pleaded with them, why am I not in a medical unit receiving treatment? My cries would go unanswered. I would remain in the psychiatric unit for weeks. My heart breaks for all those who have experienced things like this. I am not the only person in the U.S. who has undergone a misdiagnosis. Traumatic brain injuries are often misunderstood and misdiagnosed.

The nurses took turns attempting to gain access to a vein. I'm a very "hard stick." My veins have undergone far too many surgeries and procedures over my lifetime as a burn survivor, and I unfortunately have numerous medical conditions. At one point, a central line was mentioned. I was coherent enough to deny that a line be put in. For what reason? The scars left by their attempts are still visible, a reminder of the onset of cruelty that was about to head my way. This must be a bad dream. Surely, I would wake up. This couldn't be happening, right? But it was.

My daughter Hillary and grandson came to visit me, and so did my son Jarred. I was heartbroken that during their visit, I experienced another seizure. The thought of them seeing me in such a state still tears my heart. The confusion and terror that they both must have felt is palpable. My daughter would later share that I was in a state of complete psychosis; I did not recognize my children and was rambling on. They tried in vain to speak with medical staff to secure the appropriate medical treatment for me, explaining that I had a brain injury and suffered from seizure disorder. Their pleas fell on deaf ears. I was to remain in that unit, receiving treatment for a disorder I did not have, and my true medical conditions were overlooked.

My cousin, Ahlab, and eldest son, Justin, never came to the hospital; I had very little family support. It was at this point that Ahlab had informed my children not to visit me or to call the hospital. I was to find out, weeks later, that it was she who stopped all phone calls, visits, and support from my children. My personal doctor, Dr. V., attempted on two occasions to pay me a visit. She was denied access to me on both occasions; she was told by hospital staff that Ahlab had denied her visits.

During this time, she continued visiting my home to keep the house in order and care for my dogs. Ahlab forbade her to go upstairs. She found this odd; the dogs were always present, and suddenly, they were missing, yet Dr. V. could hear them crying. Finally, she forced her away around Ahlab and made her way upstairs. What awaited her was a house of horrors. Not only was the media room, office, and foyer a filthy mess, with food and trash strewn about, but the doors to the three bedrooms and the bath were closed. Dr. V. could hear the cries of Taboo and Risqué emitting from one of the rooms. She began throwing the doors open and was horrified to see my two German Shepherds, in an emaciated shape, with no food or water, covered in their own feces. She immediately took them downstairs and gave them each a bowl of food, then another, then a third. She said they ate as if they had not eaten in days. She also gave them water. They drank the bowls clean; she refilled them and let the dogs outside. She then went upstairs to clean the dog feces mess up and to clean Ahlab's mess. Ahlab had instructed Dr. V. not to clean the upstairs when I was in the hospital. Dr. V. couldn't bear the thought of me coming home to such a mess. I always kept my house in the strictest order, and she knew that I'd be disgusted not only by the trash but more so by the sight of my dogs having been locked up.

I spent five days in the first facility. I was transferred to Methodist Hospital to a unit known as 6E, an even crueler environment if you can imagine. I spent the next two weeks under their "care." I refused psychotropic medications and continued to ask for a four-day E.E.G. be performed to determine the extent of my seizure activity. No such test was ever performed. I lived in a room with the windows purposely blacked out. I was allowed to leave the room for brief periods of time. I made the occasional phone call to Ahlab, whom I had flown in from Illinois. She had, at this point, been living at my home. I pleaded with her to please help me. I trusted her to take control of all my medical and financial needs. Hours turned into days, days into weeks, and I sat and waited, hoped, and prayed that someone would come during visiting hours. Visiting hours came and went, and my name was never called. I sat alone in that dark room, wondering if I'd ever see my children and grandson again. To say nothing of the longing I had to be with my dogs. I missed them dearly. There are no words to describe the total abandonment I felt. My children were not fighting for me, and I, for the life of me, did not understand why they could have abandoned me. I was alone and utterly, totally on my own.

Finally, weeks into my stay, a doctor came to see me. I immediately identified him as being a former military officer. When you've spent as many years as I have surrounded by military members, you develop an acute awareness of those who have served. He was perplexed as to why I was hospitalized in a psychiatric unit. On our second visit, he mentioned that I should be able to be released soon. 'Soon' never came, and I decided to take matters into my own hands.

Daily, the nursing staff attempted to feed me psychotropic medications, and daily I refused. They even resorted to tricking me into taking them, stating they were seizure medications, when I knew full well they were not. I was coherent enough to foil them in these tactics. Yet, I knew that I would never see the light of day if I did not relent and take the drugs. I would need to play their game if I was ever to see the light of day again, so I did. For two days, I obediently took their pills. My plan worked. I was set for discharge the next day. Upon discharge, I was told I must sign some documents to secure my release. One of the discharge docs stated that I was bipolar, schizophrenic, and homeless. What an insult! I am none of these things, yet I signed it. I would have handed over the birthing video from my first child just to secure my freedom. (Like, I even have a birthing video!) After doing so, I was taken down to the "secret" elevator, which was the same one that had brought me up to this hellhole. I was released to my cousin Ahlab. She appeared angry that I had been discharged, I found this a bit confusing, regardless, I was overjoyed to return home to my two beloved dogs. Bobo the Cat was equally happy to see me, and I begged that the memories of that place would not visit me in my dreams. I began suffering from P.T.S.D., brought about due to my incarceration in the psych unit. These episodes, mixed with seizure activity, were deadly, and I knew it. I was terrified. I began texting my friend, Kris, a former nurse, about the times and duration of these episodes. Many were so brutal I would sometimes be knocked out by the flailing of my body. During one episode, I was showering; it seemed to go on forever. I remember reaching for the shampoo as my arms contorted and my legs buckled beneath me. There was no way out. The glass of the shower surrounded me. I couldn't walk; I was a prisoner at that moment in my own body. I could feel the pain with each blow as my arms and legs and my head hit the walls of the shower. As one bout subsided another would begin, I was a prisoner in my own body. I lay crumpled at the base of the shower; the water began to run cold. I was helpless. I prayed that it would stop. Another wave hit me, this time more violent than the last. There was nowhere to go. I lay there in a ball,my body banging against the shower walls, the water became cold, running over my still shaking body. Tears poured from my eyes, and I begged for help. My dogs were gone; there was no help. I prayed I wouldn't die there, nude, in the shower, that my daughter wouldn't be the one to find me. After what seemed like hours, it stopped. I dragged myself across the tile. Every inch seemed like a mile. Pulling my shaking and shivering body up onto the counter and then back into the bedroom. I finally made it to bed and sought refuge between the blankets. I lay there for hours. The shivering didn't stop. The fear of what had just happened and the knowledge that I would have to live like this, that I could never call 911, the reality of the whole scene rolled over in my mind. I had to remind myself that you survived.

Once home, I was happy to adjust to my new norm. My personal doctor, Dr. V., was once on board. We got down to the business of my care. She was a big part of my life, and I am eternally grateful to her. Halloween was approaching, and I wanted to do something special for my grandson. My daughter, Hillary, had made plans, and I was unable to contact my eldest son, Justin, so I spent Halloween dining out with Dr. V. I was taken back when, we drove into my neighborhood, we came across Justin, his wife Betty, and their son. Why, when I had purchased a home for them some two hours away, were they in my area trick or treating? We pulled over and greeted them. They turned away and ignored us. I was understandably hurt. It would be months before I would understand the true nature of Betty's motives.

Ahlab

I must take you back in time and share the story of Ahlab—my sweet and precious child, my cousin. Or, at least, she began that way. Innocent and pure. The product of my most beloved aunt and uncle. I was over the moon when news arrived that my aunt, who had been my former band director and had married my uncle, was pregnant with her first child. I was fifteen. I couldn't wait to hold, spoil, and gaze into the eyes of this marvel of a child. When Ahlab was born, my uncle was stationed in Virginia Beach, Virginia. I was a rebellious teenager, and it was decided that some time spent with my aunt and uncle would certainly straighten me up. I was elated to spend that summer at the beach with my favorite aunt and uncle, but most of all, with this precious child, my sweet Ahlab.

I returned home at the end of summer but never forgot the love I bore for that child. As my life progressed, I made sure Ahlab was always a part of it. I treated her as my own child. If there was a new home to enjoy or a trip to take, I included her. I dressed her in the finest clothes, purchased gifts for her, and her parents allowed her long stays at my ranch. When I had my own children, they never showed any resentment towards Ahlab; she was here first, and they accepted that. She was my much-adored cousin; it was simply a fact of life.

I was steadfast in my love and devotion to her, and there was no getting around that. I was proud of her achievements as an adult. Her first marriage was troubled. She met and married a wonderful man. He was involved in a horrific auto accident and left with a debilitating brain injury. He required care. I assumed Ahlab would have a life of caring for him, a life of servitude. I didn't understand when she decided to divorce him when he was still in a nursing care facility. I was confused by her decision, yet I felt I needed to be there for her and support her in all things. Perhaps I didn't have all the facts. I offered to listen, to be an ear, to see things through with her. To be the ever supportive older cousin. To help in any way I could. In the end, she left him. I had to support her decision. I may not have agreed with it, but I had to support it. She soon began dating several men; this concerned me. On a visit to my Pecatonica ranch, we sat and talked. I shared with her some of the downfalls and mistakes I had made earlier in my own life. She wasn't interested in listening. I had to allow her to walk her own path. I just hoped she wouldn't catch something or get in trouble with the law along the way. She was drinking a lot, going to bars, and picking up one-night stands. This was reckless behavior by anyone's standards. After a few years of this, she finally met, at a bar, one man who would change all this, Scott. A fine, upstanding man. She would go on to marry him and have two children; he purchased a home for them and was a good provider for their family. They separated, and when she denied him visitation with his children, he hung himself. I'll speak about this later in this book.

De Novo

I made some big decisions regarding my home just weeks before I experienced my seizure in October. After having spent tens of thousands of dollars on repairs to my new home, I concluded I simply needed to gut the entire interior. Painters, remodelers, landscape architects, and plumbers were hired. New flooring, windows, and all new appliances were ordered. I also did my Christmas shopping early. Neiman Marcus made a killing! I intended to spoil my cousin Ahlab, her children, and her extended family. I also had my children and my grandchildren and friends shopping completed. The dining table was piled high with my great finds at local high-end boutiques and Amazon. When I ran out of room in the dining room, I filled the closets with memorable and expensive gifts. This was going to be the best Christmas ever. The contractors pledged to have the home completed by December 15th, just in time for me to pull things together for the holidays.

I took great care in designing the new bathrooms, selecting paint colors, new light fixtures, and pulls for the kitchen. I set out for this to be the first home in Boerne to be approved by the A.D.A. (American Disabilities Association). I wanted to share it with the wounded Soldiers I had cared for over the years. With this thought process, I sat down with my designer and drew out my custom designs. The master bath would be very European, with a tub large enough for my grandson to swim in and a rain shower head in the newly expanded shower. I selected contemporary faucet fixtures that would mirror the look of a boutique hotel in Amsterdam. I added rock to the walls and flooring, new lighting, and mirrors. There would be no glass. I wanted to feel free in the shower as if it were much like the outdoor shower I had in my former home. I had a wall taken out and added windows to the bath. Fresh air is a requisite component when relaxing in the tub. The home also needed a healthy dose of color. This would only enhance my art collection, which I had surrounded myself with for countless years. In addition, I added a new HVAC system with zoned controls for the upstairs and downstairs. I planned on turning the fourth bedroom, currently a playroom for my grandson, into an art studio for him. Someplace where he could paint at will, whether on his easel or relaxing on a sofa. I wanted to introduce him to art at an early age, as I did his mother, planting the seed of creativity in his young, beautiful mind.

Another decision I made during this time was to 'gift' Taboo. I would never sell such a beloved and valuable animal. Limiting him to a quarter of an acre with a pool did not compare to the grass-filled acres with a river at my former ranch. I would still have Risqué, and she could easily be trained to be my service dog. We had a deep connection, she and I. I had two people in mind to rehome Taboo to, my former dressage trainer, Reinhardt Doersch, and Trish. Trish was a former military nurse; she was set on fire, and a box cutter was taken to her the day she returned from giving birth to her fourth son. I spoke with my importer regarding my plan, and although he was not in full agreement, I went forward with plans to rehome my beloved service dog. Taboo was not happy; he longed for the ranch, the wide-open spaces, a river to swim in, and land to roam. As did I. I had sold the ranch after losing my Friesian horse, Broer, to E.M.P., a neurological disease that is spread by possums. The medicine needed to save him was delayed by the Covid crisis. When it finally arrived, I nursed him for five days. I was devastated. I crawled into a bottle and didn't crawl out until the pain of losing my horse began to numb...

I cannot fully explain the pain of attempting to push up a 1,600-pound horse that is debilitated by such a disease. Losing my baby sister and my husband just two months apart was tough, yet I had survived. The love of family and friends brought me through and lifted me through such devastation. I did not survive the loss of Broer quite so graciously. I was heartbroken; there would be no more rides under the full moon, just he and I, down to the river, with no sounds other than the occasional fox or bobcat. Taboo was equally as distraught; he walked the fence line that bordered Broer's pasture. There was no whinny from the barn, no big black beauty in the pasture, no flowing mane of black as he ran through pastures of green. There was only silence. My broken heart fell to deep depths of despair, and in a moment, I was no longer the Silent Warrior. I was a broke woman, a widow, and a deeply heartbroken human being.

I set to the task of giving away or selling all my custom furnishings, my clothing, my hats a select portion of my art collection, the adjoining lots, and my home. Selling that place, something I had promised Randy I'd never do, was perhaps the worst mistake of my life. I made plans to move to Boerne, a move that I would later regret.

As I moved forward with my plans to rehome my dog, I spoke with Reinhardt regarding Taboo; he was upfront and honest. He had plans to move back to Europe or to Mexico, but that would not be fair to Taboo. I went with my second option, Trish. We have a love of animals in common. She is also a fellow equestrian. As deeply hard as it was, I knew that Taboo would be happier surrounded by horses with land to roam and companion dogs to play. I booked Trish a first-class ticket from Seattle to San Antonio. I also arranged for her to stay at the finest boutique hotel in Boerne. I took this opportunity to spoil her, as I so frequently did all my burn survivors.

Upon Trish's arrival, I made it clear that she needed to spend five days bonding with Taboo. He was so attached to me, never leaving my side, time would be needed for him to acclimate to his new owner. He was to stay with her at the hotel. I felt they needed that time together to bond. Several walking trails were nearby, and as Trish was a runner, I knew she and Taboo would enjoy their daily runs on the trails. I rented a luxury S.U.V. with tinted windows to transport Trish during her stay. She is a high-profile burn survivor, and I wanted to protect her and give her some anonymity during her visit.

A book signing was planned during her visit. I planned on signing my first two books, *Remarkably Intact* and *Silent Warrior*, at the event. I invited a former burn unit physician's assistant, Ricket, to join us. I knew that he would enjoy catching up with Trish and seeing how well she had recovered. The day went beautifully; we retired to my home for some more private burn survivor chats. I'll admit here, I was a bit taken back, I had not seen Ricket for some years, he had grown quite rotund and appeared older than his years. My photographer, John Mohar, was on hand and captured photos of the event. He also photographed Trish, P.A. Ricket, Ahlab and me back at my place, enjoying some time around the fire pit. Those photos include Taboo and Risqué; they would be the last photos taken of me with my beloved babies. This would also prove to be the last day I saw my dogs, November 5th, 2022.

Unbeknownst to me, Trish and my cousin Ahlab had a plan to have me arrested and put away once again in a psych unit that very evening. Thus allowing them the opportunity to remove not only Taboo but Risqué. They knew I would never agree to remove my beloved girl, Risqué. My private doctor, Dr. V., a trauma surgeon in San Antonio, caught wind of their plan and stopped me from going to the hotel with Trish that night. A "sting" had been planned at the hotel to take me into custody. Trish and Ahlab called the police and told them some wild tale about me, concocting a story that I had supposedly threatened a car dealership, and police were waiting for me at the hotel. They had every intention of arresting me. Dr. V. became aware of this plan and did not allow me to go to the hotel. She went in my place. When she arrived and was greeted by the police, she was questioned. She shared with the authorities that the story they were told could in no way be true because she had been with me the entire day. She even went so far as to offer that they view the G.P.S. in her car and see that it shows the route to my home and the time she was in my company. Trish was bloody mad; her plan had failed. She got into the back seat of Dr. V's car, slammed the door, and rang Ahlab on the way back to my house, and loudly said, "Well, the Dr. fucked that up."

Although that plan was foiled, they succeeded the next day when Trish convinced me to visit Baptist Hospital with her and expunge my medical record of the previous psychiatric unit stay. I now know there is no way to expunge a medical file, yet, at that moment, I trusted Trish and P.A. Ricket. I had no reason to doubt then. She was, after all, an R.N., currently working on her PhD. She also had me speak to P.A. Ricket. We had a long friendship dating back to 1998. I had no reason to doubt his advice or his motives in this matter. He convinced me to take

Trish's lead and go to the hospital. He spoke of a doctor who would see me there and would clear everything up. I was completely fooled. I hired a driver to take Trish and me to Baptist Hospital Stone Oak in San Antonio. After eight hours, it became obvious to me that I was about to be sent to yet another psychiatric facility. I was helpless. Trish disappeared at this point. She simply walked down the long hallway and left me. At this point, a "sitter" appeared at my door. I know all too well what that means. I was arrested and sent to yet another mental facility. I pleaded with the sitter, telling him my name and stating that I had a seizure disorder, not a mental disorder and pleaded with him to please help me. Would he please contact my family, google me, do anything. It would be three long hours before a crew arrived with a small gurney. They strapped my neck, my arms, and my legs tightly down, then loaded me into a small ambulance; I was transported to yet another in-patient facility, where once again, Ahlab would have full control of my person, not allowing my family or my doctor any visits. I was trapped. Months later, I would hear that the sitter who sat with me and heard my story did all he could to have me released; he was reprimanded and fired from his job.

My history with P.A. Ricket dates back to 1998 when I first began my volunteer work on the burn unit at Brooke Army Medical Center. I truly never noticed him. I guess he noticed me. I had a vague memory of a tall, thin P.A. roaming the halls that would occasionally cross my path. An unremarkable man, for sure. I was always too busy working with patients, doctors, and caseworkers to take note of all the staff present. He would later tell me of our chance encounters in the halls of the unit and, as he put it, just how damn lucky my husband must have been. In 2016, I believe, or it could have been 2015, Hillary and I attended the American Burn Association Conference in Boston, MA. A friend of mine had rented the Boston Aquarium for the evening and was throwing a party. It sounded like fun, so we decided to attend. Hillary and I changed into some casual clothing and headed to the event. Once there, I ran into some of the staff from the B.A.M.C. burn unit; among them stood a tall fellow; I looked at him and said, I don't know you, his response was, yes, you do, and I'm P.A. Ricket. I played along as if I did know him, but I truly didn't. He seemed to be everywhere I was that evening, it was impossible to avoid his presence. We fell into easy conversation, chatting about the unit, the war, all things "burn," you know, shop talk. Then, he took my hand, leading me to the second floor amid the octopus. The lights were dim, the colors were fascinating, and blues, greens, and vivid yellows surrounded me. The movement of the tentacles, you could almost feel them on you. Moving in a tangled web. The tall glass walls seemed to encircle me. The incline of the floor made me unsteady. As we made our way upwards, Ricket made his way closer to me. His strong, well-formed body was all over me. I was caught off guard. I was wearing a wedding ring. I had never had a man do such things. I didn't know what to do, but, I was, I was in the moment, and the moment was so damn good. He leaned down to kiss me, and it was the most passionate kiss I believe I'd ever received since I'd last kissed Randy. He was relentless, in his kissing, his pressing and his kissing. I was so confused, so caught off guard. I pushed him away and made my way down to the lower level; he followed and cornered me against the wall. Damn, what a body! This went on for nearly what seemed to be an hour. It was sublime, dangerous, and intoxicating. My entire being was as if it were in a cloud, a mist. I finally left him there, with one hell of a hard-on, to compose himself and made my way back to Hillary and the other guests.

Within half an hour, Ricket appeared at my side, buying me a drink and towering over me, possessing my space and allowing no one other than himself my time or conversation. I could smell him near me, sense his very presence. He offered to grab an Uber and take us back to our hotel. I thought twice, then accepted. Once in the Uber, he again began his advances on me. I pushed him to his side of the vehicle and made it clear that this was a simple lift back to the hotel. He walked me to my room and once again put the full-court press on me outside my door. I pleaded with him. This is all intriguing, and it's all tempting. But I'm married, you're married, and I have a daughter on the other side of that door. I pushed him off me, and the night ended there.

Over the next few days, I returned to Texas. Life at the ranch took on its lovely, sweet pace. I began receiving regular calls from Ricket. I took long rides on Broer in an attempt to rid my mind of any memory of him and the events of that night. At first, I ignored the calls, choosing to put the entire episode out of my mind, but he was relentless. I finally began taking his calls, and we struck up a friendship, I chose to call him "Mr." (like Mister). It suited him and provided a level of anonymity to our situation. Randy was working out of town, as he had since we'd been married. I was accustomed to being alone. This was the norm. I had never spoken to another man. I struggled with this. I was being unfaithful. This whole thing was wrong! Mr. said he'd like to see me, and I agreed; a date was set, and I gave him the address to the ranch.

As the day approached, I had every intention of a nice dinner in town, perhaps a glass of wine on the deck, maybe even watch the sunset, my back patio offered such stunning views of the Texas hill country, with the towering hills, encompassed by clouds, with the vivid colors, the sunsets never disappointed. That was it, my mind went no further than these thoughts. There was no way in hell he was going to get anywhere near me in the way he had attempted in the aquarium. I was too strong for that!

Well, that plan went to hell in a hand basket. I opened the door and barely welcomed Mr. into the foyer when he swept me into those sweeping arms of his and embraced me into his lips in the longest, deepest of kisses and then another. As he pressed me against the wall, my small body was no match for his, there was no way of saying no. We did make it to dinner, just barely.

Above: Last photo of Mr. and I.

Seated across from him at dinner, I could feel his energy. Each time he lifted his wine glass, I felt as if he were lifting my body, in those powerful hands of his. His eyes never strayed from me, intense, looks of passion. Then, his hand wandered to the slit on my dress and to my thigh, I could feel the heat rise up through my body, every part of me just wanted to take him home. I remained content to gaze into his eyes, listen to his stories, and continue to feel his hand on my thigh as he began to edge his hand upwards and press his fingers harder against my skin. I could literally feel the lavender oil on my legs beginning to ooze into my skin, he was digging so deep.

That evening, as we entered my bedroom, a sacred space that belonged to only myself and my husband. I became lost, I gave myself to him. With all I had. My small frame was no match for his large imposing body. If this is what melting felt like, I was certainly butter in his hands. His years of special ops training, the toned muscles, the bald head, the depth of his voice all made me tremble. My body felt a natural swoon and sway to his every movement.

My La Perla bra and panties were quickly discarded by his strong hands, and were tossed to the floor, lying there in a heap upon my dress; the sight of it was sublime. What the hell was I doing?

When he did finally place himself inside me, holding my long hair in his hands, whispering in my ear, "You're like a virgin." believe me, I felt like a virgin. It was beyond painful. I wasn't sure if I'd be able to continue. Yet, he attempted to move slowly and allow me some pleasure while pleasing himself. When it was over, I spread myself over the mass of his body, my long hair draping his chest, my legs draping his, my breath on his neck. It was beautiful. I knew this would be it. A simple interlude in this life of mine. I would never see him again. He had been honest with me about the number of affairs he had been involved in over the years, many of them involving staff at B.A.M.C. He was also honest regarding his wife, children, and grandchildren; this man loved his family. He shared with me that he was in a relationship with his wife that was loving, however, not sexual, and that for years, he had found that part of his life in other places. I knew at that moment that I was just one of many. I felt real guilt. Yet, I must live with this. It was simply another moment in life; I was simply another petal in his flower.

It's tough to face that this man would eventually go on to betray me; he would collude with Ahlab and Trish to put me away in a mental facility and had full knowledge of the theft of my dog. I will never understand such heartless behavior.

With no proper psych evaluation, I was transferred to Baptist Hospital in San Antonio. There, I would linger until I could find a way out, and find a way out, I did. I called into question my "false imprisonment," citing civil rights violations as well as patient rights violations. I also made the medical staff aware of my seizure disorder and the medication I was prescribed. After six days, I was released. A burn patient's wife, Tubbs, had her son pick me up from the hospital. It was on the way home that he informed me that in addition to Taboo leaving, Risqué was taken. I was in dismay. Where was my baby girl, and who taken her? Ahlab laid the blame directly on Trish. I'll go into detail later in this book.

Ahlab continued to live in my home. She fired my lawn service, the painter, the pool cleaning company, my housekeeper, and my personal doctor, Dr. V. She also informed my movers, Courtland and Dee that I was gone and would not be returning. They knew me far too well to believe such a story; they had only recently packed and moved my art collection and much of my personal belongings in preparation for the remodeling of the home. They became suspicious of Ahlab's motives and kept watch of the situation, as did my pool company and my doctor.

She also told everyone that I was never coming home. Telling them I was gone forever. I had left 5,124 dollars in my wallet, money that was owed to several of my staff, including Dr. V. Ahlab wrote bad checks to several of them, including 3,000 dollars due Dr. V., and kept the cash. I was to find out later, through Dr. V., that Ahlab had changed the locks on the home, thus locking her out. Ahlab had my wallet, the cash, my debit cards, frequent flyer numbers, and numerous credit cards all at her disposal while I remained locked up in the psych unit. She also helped herself to the contents of my safe. I would find out later that the combination pad had been broken. My social security card, my will, advance directives, and all financial documents were missing, as were all of my medical records. Other treasured valuables were also gone. Ahlab made a show of flashing hundred-dollar bills in front of Dr. V., and it was during this time that she offered to pay Dr. V. 5,000 dollars, with a check from my bank account, a bribe, to have Dr. V. lie. She wanted Dr. V. to lie and state that I had made terrorist threats. Thus, Ahlab would have me arrested for this, but Dr. V. flatly refused. She also attempted to sell Dr. V. several of my Christmas gifts. As you can imagine, Dr. V. was disgusted by this. Ahlab instead helped herself to all I had purchased and took my Christmas gifts with her to Illinois. I would later find out that many were given to her family and friends that coming Christmas. She also purchased a convertible car for her daughter upon arriving home in Illinois. I wonder, where does a woman with no job get the money for a car?

At some point, Ahlab became quite agitated with Dr. V., realizing that Dr. V. would not cooperate with her and that she was dealing with an ethical person on all levels. This did not fit into Ahlab's plan. In addition to changing the locks, Ahlab began filing police reports, stating that Dr. V. had stolen my refrigerator; in another, she stated that Dr. V. had stolen jewelry from my home. When the Boerne police rang Dr. V. regarding these reports, she kindly offered to have them search her home. They declined.

During the time that Ahlab resided in my home, she contacted a realtor to fire-sell my home in addition to contacting an estate sale company to sell my art collection, clothing, and any other valuables she did not avail herself of. She did all this by obtaining an illegally gotten power of attorney. How she came about acquiring this document is a story unto itself. I was home from the hospital just the night before when Ahlab announced I'd need to accompany her down to the attorney's office and sign a legal, medical power of attorney. I was so out of it and still in a great deal of shock. I had also taken psychotropic medications to get myself out of the unit I had been on. Believing, of course, that my beloved cousin was there to provide the best care for me. We met with Ned, the attorney and his associate, Adder. I was presented with a document. When I insisted that it be a medical power of attorney only and not a full power of attorney, I was told it was just that. I was not allowed to review the document. I was rushed through the signing process and whisked out the door. What I had just signed was a full power of attorney. I would find out the full extent of their deception later.

This document, eventually acquired by me with the help of Dr. V., is chilling. In it, she takes away all my rights and gives herself full ownership of my estate. She also names one of my former burn patient's wives, Tubbs, as the successor should anything happen to her. The document was drawn up by an attorney, Ned, that I had hired to help me expunge my medical file. This same attorney was assisted by my late baby sister, Audra, and me during his addiction to cocaine. I had to face the fact I had been betrayed by a family member, Ahlab, the wife of a burn survivor (who had benefited greatly from the Moonlight Fund) Tubbs, a burn survivor Trish, a former burn unit medical attendant P.A. Ricket, and the attorney I trusted, Ned. It would be months before I truly understood all that had happened, and that would prove to be too late to stop the damage that was done, and what was about to befall me.

They would later use this document to justify the theft of my property, including the dogs and the items from my home. It is a felony, a federal offense, to use a POA, to steal items from anyone, particularly a person that is disabled or elderly.

Once home from my second stint in a psych unit, Ahlab acted quickly to have me committed once again. I awoke to a beautiful Saturday morning, happy to be home, free from the terrors of a mental hospital. I announced to Ahlab that I'd like to take her shopping and do lunch at one of my favorite restaurants. I loved spoiling her! I was unable to find my seizure medication, and it was at this point that she assured me, "You don't really need those, do you? I'll be with you; there is nothing to worry about." During a shopping spree for her family, I was choosing a few items for her and her family when I experienced a seizure. I had been gazing at the snow globes at one of my favorite boutiques; I love watching the snow as it glides to the ground in scenes of winter wonderland. I remember thinking this would make for a lovely gift for Ahlab's parents. Perhaps it may remind them of my mother. We lost her to cancer in 2015. She was the older sister to Ahlab's father. The seizure hit, and I stepped back from the display. My eyes searched for Ahlab. I needed her love and support at that moment. What happened next was a nightmare. I remember Ahlab taking my arm and leading me out of the store. I would later discover, through police reports, that she had called the police. My seizure continued in front of the store; a crowd had gathered. I was in no shape to feel the embarrassment at the time that would come later. The police arrived, placed handcuffs on me tightly behind my back, questioned me and treated me as if I were a criminal, as I continued having a seizure. They placed me in the back of the squad car for all to see, and left the scene. For a full twenty minutes, this played out in front of a crowd. This entire humiliating scene. The only memory I have is of looking into Ahlab's eyes and saying, "What have you done to me?'

The police took me to our local emergency room. Ahlab did not accompany me; instead, she reentered the store, purchased the snow globes with my credit card, jumped into the luxury SUV I had rented for her, and returned to my home, where she would enjoy the food and libations I had purchased for her stay.

This time, I was transferred back to University Hospital, where I would remain for the next five days. I experienced the same disdain and poor treatment offered at the previous facility. However, I will say it was not the previous unit, 6E that I had been on. This unit was much more humane, and I met a doctor and a nurse practitioner there who truly believed in me and understood my brain injury and the seizures caused by it. They hinted at concerns regarding Ahlab, yet I was still oblivious to her motives and her end goal. My doctor took me aside; he had several documents in his hands and asked me, point blank, "How well do you know your cousin?" He told me that I could go home on Wednesday if I took my anti-seizure medications and experienced no seizures for three days. He gave me his word. He was true to his word, and I went home that Wednesday. I was deemed competent by the psych medical staff and returned home. I called Ahlab and gave her this news. She seemed distant and angry. I could not for the life of me understand why; this was certainly good news, was it not?

I had never been anything but kind to Ahlab, just a few years earlier, when she made the decision to undergo gastric bypass surgery, I supported her decision. I was also supportive when she gained the weight back and listened intently to her struggles. I never gave my cousin any reason to dislike me, I showed her love and true compassion.

This was the fateful ride home when Tubbs's son picked me up from the hospital. It was during the ride home that I was told that my dog, Risqué, had been given away. I spoke with Ahlab on the phone and asked how she could possibly do such a thing; how and why would she give away my beloved animal. Her only response was... "I thought you were never coming home, and I needed to get rid of the dog."

I sat the rest of the way home in a state of shock and confusion. I would soon be home. There would be no reunion with my treasured and much-beloved dogs. Who would protect me? Take me to the bathroom at night? Guide me to the kitchen, love me? Detect my seizures? They were gone, and my heart skipped a long, languid beat.

I was in such shock that I didn't notice that the Christmas gifts were missing from the dining table and that the closets had been ransacked. The safe lock was also left hanging, broken. All I could do was grieve. I walked about like I was in a trance. Where was my dog? Where had she gone? Ahlab suddenly wanted to change her ticket and get back to her children early. I complied and got online to change her ticket; even then, I didn't notice that someone had gained access to my computer. My personal files were a mess. Not only on the computer but stacks upon stacks of my files, the Moonlight Fund files were lying everywhere. I simply didn't see it. I was in a state of utter shock. Ahlab stated she'd need extra luggage. I complied and told her to take whatever she needed. I gave no thought to this. I also gave no thought to her leaving early. In retrospect, it was all so obvious, yet, at the time, my mind was so fragile, so damaged, I could not think straight. Ahlab left early. She left with suitcases full of my things and a wallet full of cash. She left with the confidence that I was weak and fragile and that she was going to take control of my life, my assets, and my complete future.

I would later find that Ahlab was secretly doing all she could to have me committed to a state mental hospital for life. This would have been the death of me. I'm a strong, independent, and free spirit. Putting me away would have been a death sentence. She had also informed my children to stay out of the picture, stating that she had full control and that they should not be involved. However, she asked my daughter if she might find a good nursing home with maximum security. She was willing to offer this as a second choice to the state facility. I believe she did this to keep Hillary compliant and quiet. By the grace of the Gods, Hillary saw through her charade and played along to gather more information and set about releasing me from this troubling situation. At the same time, Ahlab and Tubbs threatened my daughter, stating that if she made any contact with me, she would risk losing custody of her child. I also had firsthand knowledge of Dr. V; this would prove to be invaluable. In addition, my pool company, painter, movers, friends, family, and many others who watched Ahlab and her co-conspirators at work were keeping notes. State Farm Insurance was also quietly gathering their own evidence in this case. All were silently watching this tangled web. Best to sit back and allow them to hang themselves.

The signs were all there, yet I did not see them. Ahlab had dyed her hair the same color as mine. She sent me a long list of major items to purchase for her home, including a new hot water heater. She also made several demands for large sums of cash. In addition, she asked that I purchase her new appliances, including a new washer and dryer. My children saw these lists, and it caused them some concern; they cared not that I should be spending the money; what they cared about was the way in which she was asking; it was more of a demand than an ask. My son was wise and decided to screenshot the numerous demands she texted to my phone. She was becoming bold in her demands. I felt an obligation to help her. She did have my baby sister's daughter in her care. When I purchased the washer and dryer, she insisted that they be identical to the ones I owned, down to the model number and color. She made sure to tell me that she had purchased the same detergent that I used. All odd behaviors, yet I had no clue. All I could do was please her, but enough was never enough. The demands got bigger and bolder.

I also found clues regarding Ahlab's deeds on my computer while I was put away. She was using my .org email as her own. We found emails from her to the attorney, Ned, that I hired on my computer, using my email. It was obvious, he had now become her attorney. She detailed in this correspondence how she was letting my staff go, one by one. People who had worked for me for numerous years were told they no longer had a job. My painter had planned on being a part of the renovations and repainting the entire home, as had several of my long-time contractors. They would later tell me that Ahlab informed them I was never coming home. My pool guy was very uncomfortable with what was going on and remained faithful to servicing my pool in my absence. I'm grateful that my pool company saw through the fake emails and sensed danger. The information they would later share would be bone-chilling.

I would later be told, by my lawn guy, my doctor and painter, that Ahlab had referred to them as "wetbacks", refused to pay them the money owed, threatened them with all sorts of outlandish, crazy things, to have them deported, arrested, and more. It breaks my heart. These were all good, faithful staff, that had been by my side for years. I feel heartsick that they had been drawn into this sick and twisted drama.

I had left my wallet with Ahlab with instructions to use the five thousand plus dollars in it to pay my staff, including my lawn guy, the painter, and Dr. V. She kept the cash and wrote out several bad checks. This caused many problems for me down the road. When I did return home, I needed to pay back everyone who had received a bad check. What a mess. Perhaps this is how she was able to purchase the convertible car for her daughter once she arrived home in Illinois.

She had also hacked into every social media account, both public and private sites, and accessed all my documents. My desk and each cabinet in the home had been gone through. Every legal document I had at the house was lying in a stack near my computer. My medical files, all kept in the safe, were gone. The signs of a good ransacking were evident. She made notes on several documents; we would later find these notes, telling clues as to her true intentions.

Perhaps the most heart-wrenching thing I saw was upstairs. Ahlab had been sleeping in the media room on my sectional, it was covered in stains; and the entire area was a mess. Empty beer bottles were littered about, with candy wrappers and chip bags strewn on the floor. It was as if homeless people had been there for years, the smell was putrid. The bathroom was disgusting; I have never seen such filth in my life. But nothing prepared me for what I was about to catch sight of as I opened the doors to the adjoining three bedrooms. There were dog feces everywhere. Risqué never had any accidents, and by the looks of it, this was a dog in distress. My dog had apparently been locked in the bedrooms for long periods of time and had diarrhea while I was locked away. My heart broke. How could anyone be so cruel to a defenseless animal? In that moment, I felt rage, very real rage.

At that moment, I was happy Ahlab was gone. I'm not sure what I would have done. I would have screamed at the top of my lungs, "how could you?!!!" How anyone could take an animal that was accustomed to being by their owner's side twenty-four-seven, whether it be indoors or out in the yard, and lock her up? I can't imagine how my poor dog felt. With me gone and having to be locked in a bedroom, she must have been a wreck. The pain I felt was palpable. Ahlab had gone too far. Her cruel nature towards animals was on full display. This was evil, on a whole new level, and something I had never witnessed before.

In addition, I paid a visit to my bank; they had begun an investigation into just who was monitoring my personal bank accounts and those of my foundation, the Moonlight Fund, during my stay in the hospital. They shared with me the paper records showing a ping originating from a local number. It was one thing to attempt to destroy and deceive me. When you mess with the Moonlight Fund, I had to draw a hard line in the sand and vow to protect the fund and its assets. The bank also had a video of Ahlab entering the bank on several occasions. I spoke with my personal banker, Jason, and he felt it best I move my personal funds out of my accounts to another bank and keep the Moonlight Fund intact at his branch. I made plans to do just that; unknowingly, I informed Ahlab's attorney, Ned, of my plan. I was, at this point, oblivious to all they were doing. He insisted on being at the bank when I was withdrawing the funds, and Tubbs showed up at the same time. We ran into her in the private banking lobby; she certainly does not have the money to have a private banker. Why on earth was she there? It was all far too coincidental. Yet, I was still unaware that these were the enemies, and I missed the obvious signs of what they were doing.

I continued to trust Ahlab and believe all she said. After all, she was my much-adored little cousin, the daughter of my most treasured aunt and uncle. I thought so much of her that after the death of my own baby sister who left behind a seven-year-old daughter, Trynn, that I waived custody of and told the state of Illinois that my niece should be awarded to my cousin, Ahlab. A mistake. Something I would in the future regret.

Allow me to segue here. In America and across the globe, there exists a common thread: a deadly and costly battle arises among family members, friends, and those associated with people compromised by age, health issues, and the loss of their spouse. It's called guardianship. As you'll come to read in this book, Ahlab used my brain injury, my seizure disorder, the loss of my husband, my wealth, and my generosity against me. She laid out a well-devised plan and involved other parties, those people whom I'd also been quite generous to, a burn survivor, the wife of a burn survivor, a former burn unit staff member, and an attorney I had trusted with my business. The goal, well, it was always control of my money. By seizing my person, they would then seize control of all my assets, my home, bank accounts, life insurance, book revenues, household goods, my art collection, and more. She worked over the period of 17 months, and she was relentless in her efforts, but in the end, I stood my ground, and I won. I did so from a jail cell, one she had put me in. It's a twisted, long and languid tale, one I will not go into here. You'll have to read further to grasp the enormity of the situation. My point is anyone, at any time, who you trust the most can and may betray you. In my case, they did.

My bank made me aware that my accounts were "pinging." They also had video footage of Ahlab and Tubbs entering the bank. With this knowledge, we decided it best to move some assets to another bank.

I made the journey to my other bank, knowing I had accounts there I'd not accessed in years. I assumed I had only two accounts that I could place the six-figure cashier's check into. I was a bit surprised when the banker informed me that I had four accounts, two solely in my name and two joint accounts with my late husband, Randy. I knew immediately that I needed to deposit the money into the joint accounts and protect what collateral I had left. The account of a deceased person cannot be seized. Once again, I felt Randy was looking after me from above, offering me a safe haven and an account that Ahlab and her posse could not access. Ned, the attorney whom I still believed to be a friend and whom I had previously hired to represent me, was, in fact, already working with Ahlab. The five-thousand-dollar retainer I paid him was being used against me, not for my benefit. He inquired about the new accounts; it was at this point that I became suspicious of him and his motives. When I responded to his inquiry with the knowledge that I had placed the funds into a joint account, he replied that it must be a paid-on-death account and that I would still have the ability to give Ahlab access. He had the P.O.A. that I had signed and fully intended to use that to access any funds I had and give Ahlab those funds, thus giving himself a payday. I informed him that Randy and I had no P.O.D. accounts. We never planned on him dying. When we discovered he had brain cancer, the furthest thing from our minds was money and how accounts were set up. All we were focused on was spending what little time he had left together. Life is precious, and I loved that man.

It wasn't until Dr. V. came to me and shared all she knew that I became aware of Ahlab's plan to seize all my assets, take control of my estate, and have me committed to a state mental hospital. She also shared that Ahlab had attempted to sell her several of the Christmas gifts I had purchased and left behind in the home. Dr. V. flatly refused. She played along only to gain access to information, and Ahlab was dumb enough to share. Ahlab was a fool. She had a plan, a sick and twisted plan, to separate me from my children, my assets, and my future. To put me away permanently, to secure a do not resituate order on me, and to have me put on psychotropic medications while removing my seizure medications. This was a diabolical plan, yet she felt confident; she had allies, one of whom was an attorney; she felt powerful, and she felt she'd win.

We discovered that not only did Ahlab want to become "Celia Belt," but she was also set on destroying the real Celia Belt. Her cunning did not stop at assets and my person; she also took control of my five public sites on Facebook, including those directly related to the Moonlight Fund and my personal page. In addition, she hacked into my computer and used my ".org" email to correspond with Ned, the attorney. They, Ahlab, Tubbs Trish, and Ned were setting the stage; all were eager to profit from putting me away and taking away the key. In numerous conversations with Dr. V., Ahlab stated that she was the ghostwriter of my books and would be writing future books. I have never used a ghostwriter and never will. This is sick on a whole new level.

We would later gather numerous documents from the police showing that reports had been made and phone calls received from Ned, Trish, Tubbs, and Ahlab. They were continually calling the police and stating that I was delusional, that the dogs were truly not "missing," and that I needed to have wellness checks made at my home. This led to me being harassed by the police. My contractors were constantly protecting me, stating, "Miss Celia, hide." Friends, spending a pleasant evening at my home, found themselves at the mercy of a police raid; the home would be searched for what? For no apparent reason. This was all getting very out of hand. I was subjected to constant visits by the police. They were simply doing their job; they had to act on these calls. It did, however, become brutal in nature, as you will read in this book.

Ahlab could have had it all. She had given up work knowing I would support her as long as she cared for my niece, I would support her, both financially and emotionally. Between me and what she received from social security, she would lead a comfortable life. She got greedy; she wanted it all. She had set her sights on our aunt, a multimillionaire. She is an incredible businesswoman who made her fortune shortly after her daughter, my cousin Keena Rothhammer, swam in the Munich Olympics. Ahlab felt she had endeared herself to Aunt Dianne to the point she would be named in her will. She spoke of this often. In fact, I took it for granted that Ahlab would continually state, "When Aunt Dianne dies." I thought nothing of it. She would say it so often, it became the norm. In retrospect, now that I know what I know, she was just waiting for my aunt to pass so she could collect. She flat-out assumed it would be a payday for her and her children. How disturbing. For someone to think of a family member's passing in such a way, yet I did not see it as a sign of trouble. When my uncle, her father, returned from a trip to visit his sister Dianne in New Zealand, he informed Ahlab that she was, in fact, not named in Dianne's will and that Aunt Dianne was, in fact, naming her three children and her grandchildren in her will. That's when Ahlab set her sights on me. I may not yet have had the money Aunt Dianne had, but I was the obvious second choice. I was so naïve; I didn't see the writing on the wall. I was a fool, and fools fall hard.

I'm eternally grateful to my late husband Randy, my friends, my burn survivors, D.A.R. Members, the airshow community, military members, Dr. V., and the Gods for the strength to survive and fight back. I am a burn survivor, and surviving is what I do best. I would need my spirit guides, my friends, and all those who believe in me, for the fight I was about to fight would be the biggest battle of my life. I cannot express the number of times I cried to the heavens, "It's not real; this has got to be a bad dream! She didn't do this to me!" Yet, she did.

I knew I needed help recovering Risqué; it was at this point that I was contacted by Copper Star Investigations. I knew the owner, Rocky Davis, and it felt like a great fit. They would go on to discover that Ahlab had a history of failed businesses, bankruptcies, and much more; they would also find that Tubbs had foreclosed on two properties. In addition, they shared much information regarding Trish. I was shocked. I had no idea. As they told me I was dealing with people that were expert at conning others, I sat in disbelief. Could this all be true? Could this possibly be happening?

I had the continual thought that I must forgive them. Everyone that came to hurt me in one way or another deserves my forgiveness. Isn't that what Jesus did on the cross? His last words were words of forgiveness, as will be mine.

Voile

I was finally home, aka, as I call it, C.B.'s White Trash Bed & Breakfast! Things were a mess. The contractors were far behind schedule. I didn't even have a bed to sleep in. I slept on the floor, as I had for months. I had given away the furniture and appliances I'd purchased for the home two years earlier. I was starting anew, a fresh start. This house has been a nightmare. The previous owners of the home had covered up the buckling flooring with furniture and rugs. I discovered this as my movers were moving me just two years ago. A bad foundation, leaking roof, and faulty electrical, non-working pool equipment...need I say more? This was back in 2021. I was in a mess, and I knew it. I fell so many times over the buckled flooring that my knees have permanent hematomas. Taboo saved my life more than once. At least I had my dogs, Bobo the Cat, and my dear friend, Bethany, to see me through. Back then, I began to drink heavily to numb all the pain. The loss of the ranch, my horse, my sister, and, of course, my love, my Randy. I grew so ill and weak that I required hospitalization for low potassium to restore my good health. I thank the gods for Bethany, my true friend; she was by my side for those dark days. I fell so deep into despair that I didn't know which way was up. I decided to shut down the Moonlight Fund, at least as a non-profit, and privatize it, thus making it a private foundation. That was the one sane decision I made.

I had to pull myself up from my bootstraps, admit to my poor decisions, and move forward. I was a grandmother too, my Remington, I love him dearly. What legacy would I leave him if I continued in such a state?

I did just that, I got my shit together, and I'm proud that I got to the point of completely gutting this mess of a house. So, here I was, nearly two years later, walking into a home that was, quite honestly, trashed. Yet, I was free. I was out of the psych units. I could move forward with the renovations and assess my losses.

Ahlab was gone; however, she didn't leave empty-handed. Little by little, I discovered things that were missing from the home. My wallet was empty, my credit cards were gone, and a call to my credit card companies confirmed the worst. My identity was stolen. My safe had been broken into; missing were my social security card, my will, my medical records, and advance directives. My clothing, all housed in wardrobes in the garage, meticulously packed by my movers, had been rummaged through. I looked in the closet for my Louis Vuitton bags that produced nothing, they were all gone. I'll never know what she left or what she took. My Christmas presents, all purchased early in preparation for the holidays, were also missing. Each and every gift would never be given. She had helped herself to all she saw fit.

When I realized she had not only taken my valuables but also my name and my identity. I discovered lewd emails from Ahlab to men using my email and hijacked photos of myself. Keep in mind that my cousin weighed in excess of several hundred pounds on a good day. She was posting my photos on dating sites and using my '.org' email address to not only converse with my pool company, the attorney Ned, whom I thought was "my" attorney, she had working for her at this point, with funds I had paid him, but also those men she met on dating sites. I was disgusted. I had enough. I took the long side braid I had fashioned on the side of my neck and cut my hair off. As I was doing so, my painter, Armando, arrived for work that day, screaming out, "Miss Celia, No!!!" Your beautiful hair!!" I took nearly two feet of braided hair and threw it out the front door. If she wanted my identity ... she can have it! That's the Native American blood in me and a bit of my Nordic blood. My long, lustrous mane had been my identity for my entire life. It was gone, laying there, on the front walkway, a mass of red.

I had to pick up the pieces of a shattered life. Ahlab had threatened my daughter with C.P.S. custody of her child should she be found at my house. Her partner, Tubbs, did the same. What was she to do? She was terrified. She had two educators telling her she'd lose her son if she visited her mother or was observed at her mother's home. Both of these women should lose their education licenses for such threats. The grief my daughter must have felt is indescribable. She is an extraordinary mother, daughter, sister, and friend to a select few. How they threatened her and the torment that they offered is unthinkable. They have taken away from me the thing that meant the most: time and visits with my beloved grandson and daughter. Hillary was afraid to be around me, afraid to have her son near me. She was terrified of what Ahlab might do next. Ahlab was winning. She was separating me from my family.

With me in a psych hospital, they had full control, and they were dead set on destroying Hillary's life as well as mine. Nasty text messages from Ahlab began to arrive on Hillary's phone, threatening her. Stating she had better stay away from her mother. Hillary desperately sought the help of my two sons, Justin and Jarred. They were equally confused and frightened by recent events; both chose not to help their sister. Not out of any lack of care, for they were also confused and frightened by the actions of Ahlab. That did not stop Hillary; she knew in her heart that she must help her mother, but she did not know how she would do so.

It was around this time that police officers began regular visits to my home. Ahlab and the members of her "posse'" Trish, Tubbs, and Ned, were calling them to request wellness checks. These checks became abusive, as you will later realize in this book. My sub-contractors, my friends, my family, and my person were all harassed, and I was eventually assaulted by police officers. I lay no blame on the local police; they were misinformed, misguided, and were simply doing what they thought was their job. Yet, brutality is not necessary.

One night, in mid-December, I heard a noise as I lay sleeping in the living room. As I rose, I saw a man near the pool. I did what came instinctively to me. I flung open the door and shouted, "Back, back!" with my arms in military defense mode. I swear he was over the back fence in two strides. I thought he moved like Sasquatch—damn, he was fast. I came back into the house. Gathering my thoughts, I decided I had best make a police report. I rang the local police department. Two officers were dispatched to my home. I explained to them what I had seen: an intruder on my property and my need to make a report. They brushed off the conversation and barely used their flashlight to look out back when suddenly, they were all over me, throwing me into handcuffs behind my back. I cried out, why, why are you doing this to me? They stated they were taking me in. I stood my ground, stating that they were in violation of my civil rights as a U.S. citizen. My home was stacked with boxes of household goods the movers had previously packed. This proved to be a hazardous place to be tossed about. I was thrown against many boxes for quite some time, yelling at me, things that meant absolutely no sense and had nothing to do with my call. I had bruises on my arms and legs and gashes on both. The scars are still visible to this day. I was bleeding, and the pain did not end there. They dragged me out of my home on a cold and rainy night, with no shoes on my feet and no jacket to protect me from the cold rain. Once in their squad car, the two officers began to talk about me in a derogatory way. Although I lost much of my hearing in my riding accident, I can still read lips, even from the side. I asked that they refrain from talking about me. They were at first a bit dismayed that I knew the context of their conversation, but they eventually discontinued it. They took me to the local emergency room. Not for the injuries sustained at their hands but to be evaluated for possible admission into yet another psych unit.

Here we go again. I repeatedly asked both officers for their badge numbers; both declined to share said information with me. I also asked for a copy of the report. I was never given that also. Both officers hung around the E.R. for several hours. Gloating over the fact they had "brought in" Celia Belt in. At one point, I finally confronted both officers, once again asking for their badge numbers and a copy of the report. Both were denied to me. I had had enough, this needed to end! At that point, I looked at the younger officer—he had inflicted most of my wounds—and I said, "Do you know what a rattlesnake does when it's skinned? It still feels... I'm going to skin you..." I then looked at the older officer, and although he had inflicted no harm, he nonetheless watched... and I said to him, "Who do you love the most?" Needless to say... my comments were never reported...Now, I could have been charged for both these comments with threats to a police officer, yet they were never reported. Both officers left with a look of terror on their faces. If my mother were alive and knew I had uttered such words to police officers, I would have received one hell of an ass whooping!

I asked Officer Swift, of Boerne P.D. be brought to the scene to assist me while in the E.R.. She had been involved with previous calls to my home. She had empathy for her, and I felt I could trust her. She arrived shortly thereafter and stayed for several hours. She viewed the bruises on my arms and legs. She remained at the hospital for several hours. My daughter had already been contacted by Officer Swift and arrived with fresh clothing for me to take to whatever facility they were planning on sending me to. Well, you know what happened. I spoke with that facility, and after our twenty minute conversation, they deduced that I was not in need of psychiatric care and I should be released to my home. I called a driver and returned home to resume my work on the house.

The day after, Officer Gomez visited my home and filed report # B2205344. I showed him my bruises and bloodied arms and legs. He called the station and informed me that the report would need to be taken at the station. I took his advice. I spoke with my personal doctor, Dr. V., and she suggested it best that she should accompany me, as well as Courtland and Dee, to provide me with three witnesses to the reporting of the incident.

Two days later, accompanied by Dr. V., my movers, Courtland and Dee, and I went to the local police department to make a report. Upon entering the police department, we were greeted by a very large officer. He stated that I could make the report upstairs and that my three companions could wait for me in the lobby. I flatly refused. I insisted that they be present during the making of my report. I would not be separated from my witnesses during the taking of this report. We got a great deal of pushback from the officer, but I wouldn't budge. The officer finally complied and led us upstairs. We entered a room and took our seats. He took the two-and-a-half-hour report. Report #B2205423. I asked if he'd like to take photos of my bruises and bloody gashes. He declined, stating there was no need for that. He rose and excused himself to make copies of the report for me. It took four tries for him to get it right; each time, there were errors in the report that we caught and asked for corrections to be made. In the end, he handed Dr. V. an unsigned copy of the report. He did ask if I needed anything; my only response was, "A cup of coffee would be nice," and wouldn't you know... he stated they were out of coffee. As we exited the building, we came across a housekeeper diligently going about her tasks, and guess what she had ... coffee.

As we exited the building, Courtland and Dee looked at one another and said that the report would go right in the trash. I couldn't believe their words. How could a report of police brutality, with three witnesses and a woman with visible bruises and bloodied areas still showing and an E.R. visit with records, to say nothing of a well-respected personal doctor on site, be dismissed? Surely, this would be taken seriously. I waited for a follow-up call; surely, a detective would want to speak with me and gather more evidence. Certainly, this was a civil rights violation. Certainly, as a resident of Boerne, this fine, upstanding community, a widow in her own home alone, my rights would be protected. Surely.

There were no calls. I would later find out that the report was never investigated. It had been dropped. Case closed. I would also find out, months later, that the case I filed regarding my missing dog had been closed. In addition, the report for the theft of property from my home was also–case closed. Where is the justice? Is there none?

I must pause here and pay tribute to a hero, a Warrior before her time, Miss Rosa Parks. In 1955, she sat on a bus in Montgomery, Alabama, and said one word to a police officer; that word was "NO." She changed the course of civil rights as we know it with that one word; with her courage and her will to stand, she made her voice heard, regardless of the danger it presented to herself and those she loved. I must be just as fearless here as I was dragged through my home, citing my civil rights, looking down at my bloodied and soon-to-be bruised arms and legs. What was I taking a stand for? I was a woman, alone in her home, a widow, a brain injury survivor, a burn survivor, and a survivor of abuse. What was I standing for when I recited my civil rights to those police officers? To be honest with you ... I don't know; it was simply a gut reaction. I forgive those officers. For whatever reason, which I don't know, they were overly rough with me. I posed no threat. I was non-combative, yet I had to endure it, all of it.

As the holidays approached, I was faced with spending Christmas alone, with no gifts, and a family that feared being anywhere near me. My friend, Venomara, had sent over a fully decorated tree for me. That was all I had. It was beautiful. Thankfully, my incredible movers, who had become like family, invited me to spend Christmas with them. I hastily found plenty of incredible gifts for each of them and their family members. This included some Louis Vuitton items I'd never used that I was sure their wives would appreciate. I was thankful that Ahlab did not find all my Louis bags! Wrapping each carefully with incredible bows and intricate tie-ons, I did this with the love I felt for them. This was not an easy task. I was still in a great deal of pain from my roughing up by the police. It was painful to look down at the still visible gashes on my arms and hands, with the knowledge that the police had inflicted these wounds. I was raised to respect and trust the police, this was all so confusing. I sent the gifts home with each of my movers in preparation for the big day. I was excited; the house was still a mess, and I was continuing to sleep on the floor, but I would have Christmas! Then, for no apparent reason, my movers informed me they were rescheduling Christmas. What? Rescheduling Christmas? That's like a cop without coffee. So, I went to plan B and made arrangements to spend the day with my good friend, Doris Hensley. I'd met D, as I call her when I hired her to be my driver. We quickly stuck up a friendship, and I cherish her to this day. I packed games, magazines, my military slang dictionary, and some nice champagne. All were arranged in a box with my toiletries; a box was all I had as my luggage was packed away. Something happened, and to this day, I can't tell you what took place. I have no memory of Christmas; the box lay on the stairs right where I had placed it. Its contents had not been touched. My son Jarred and his wife Vanessa came by on Christmas day to drop off my gifts and pay me a visit. I was nowhere to be found. I guess that will be one of my questions when I meet the Gods... What happened to Christmas 2022?

I can only speculate that my brain, dealing with so much trauma, had simply shut down, in some form or fashion, protecting me. This would not be an unusual thing to happen for someone that has sustained multiple traumatic events. I had been dealing with so much, head on, and I believe that my mind simply needed a break from all the terror it had been put through.

I would later discover that the reign of terror and theft that began with my cousin, Ahlab, spread like wildfire. Those close to me, some of whom I trusted, would begin stealing from me. I became an easy target. I was so compromised. I was weak. My whole being was focused on Ahlab, on getting my dog back that others saw an opportunity and they took it. So, they stole from me also. I would find out much later that many of the people I had trusted stole from me and took what was not theirs. Disheartening, to say the least.

Boerne, Texas

I first moved to Boerne back in 2002. Hillary found a sixteen-acre place with two homes on it and a barn. The century-old oaks, in excess of four hundred, were calling my name like a siren. They were in need of a good arborist, and this place, with its twelve-foot-wide rickety gate and three-mile winding road that led to a 1950s rock home, was just perfect in every way. It needed me as much as I needed it. It was ideally suited for me, my daughter, and my horse, and the guest house was perfect for my son to visit when he was home during weekends off at Baylor University. I also had the thought of cleaning up the guest house and renting it as a B and B. This could and did provide some extra income.

Above: With my first two Friesians, Broer and Merlin in Boerne, Texas.

I had divorced Dick (D.J. as he prefers to be called) just the year before, and although he was an incredibly wealthy man, I asked for nothing other than four thousand dollars a month for two years. I also asked that he continue to cover the expense of the children's prep school tuition. He agreed. I left the millionaire lifestyle behind. Don't get me wrong, not that I didn't appreciate his kindness and generosity; I simply didn't offer him the love that he deserved, and that's not right in anyone's book. What was important to me was that he remained a father figure in the lives of my children at any cost, which was of utmost importance to me. He was the only father Hillary had ever known. The bond they shared was so special, and you can't put a price on that.

So, here I was, single again, running the Moonlight Fund, pro-bono, working this rough piece of land. I took a job at a beer saloon, Leon Springs Dance Hall, some twenty-five miles away; that way, I could train horses by day and drive Hillary the thirty-plus miles to school and get her to dance classes. It was the only place that would hire me. Each time I filled out an application, potential employers would look down at my application, which included National Sales Manager, General Management, Commercial Real Estate Broker, Non-Profit Founder, etc., and recipient of numerous national awards, etc., and none would take me seriously. I just needed a bust-ass job that would help pay the bills. I had fence posts to buy and mouths to feed. I was back in the days of my childhood. I was in survival mode. I was so relieved when the manager at Leon Springs gave me that job. Each night, I'd grab an hour or two of sleep, jump into my Ford 250 Diesel truck, and take the long drive down to Leon Springs to work my shift. I was still tired from working horses, driving

Hillary to a private school in San Antonio, dance classes in the evening, and volunteering on the burn unit, but it was necessary.

I never dreamed I'd bring home the cash that I ended up raking in. This new, steady cash flow allowed me to build new fencing, thus allowing me to board more horses. I had a reputation in the horse world. Horses that were "problem" horses, dangerous horses, were brought to me for work. Through love and patience, these horses and I developed an understanding, and I had great success. I could look into the eyes of a horse, spend time with him, and be the first to back him within days; I loved this part of me. my spirit. This provided me with a source of income. We sustained ourselves this way for two years, and then I began dating a truly kind and sincere pulmonologist from San Antonio.

We married the next year, and he helped make so many of my "horse dreams" come true. He built me a full-blown equine center on my property, a show barn with an attached arena, and upgraded the pastures. What I didn't count on was the attention importing the Friesians and building a show barn would bring me. I'd find cars lined up on the street, taking photographs of me riding. Numerous articles were written about my importing the breed into the States; this attracted much unwanted attention. I found myself riding at night, using the lights in the arena, simply to find some peace. I brought something that was considered "big" to the area. Boerne was a small town back then, a dot on the horizon, a main street with just one antique shop, and a coffee shop that had been in the same family for three generations. The police followed you home at night, not to harass you but to care for you, and the librarian knew you by name. That was the Boerne I loved. It's not the Boerne I moved back to in 2021. It is now the second fastest-growing city in the State of

Texas. In a world of boutique hotels, high-end shopping, and fine dining, the old timers have left or died, and it has lost its way.

Audra Starr

I was twelve when my baby sister was born. My parents allowed me to name her. I chose a name after one of my favorite television female heroines in the series The Big Valley, Audra. Linda Evans played the part of a stunning woman, an excellent horse person, and a great spirit. I was over the moon that my parents allowed me such an honor. My father reserved her middle name, which would be Starr, for the stars are always bright and look down on us from the heavens forever. I can still remember the day when I awoke to see the paper with the footprints on it and the name Audra Starr VanBibber above it. From that day on, she was my baby and my love.

I spent much of my childhood adoring her and the better part of my teen years in foster homes. I chose to live in foster homes; the abuse, or in those days, we called it discipline, at home was tough. After my father left us, my Nordic mother ruled with an iron fist. She was doing the best she could, getting her degree and raising three children on her own. It couldn't have been easy. I was a handful, for sure. This, combined with my younger brother and a young daughter, the responsibility must have been daunting. As I placed myself into foster care, my separation from Audra was more painful than anything I had ever experienced. I went months without seeing her. This was my mother's way of punishing me for seeking out foster care. I understand. When I finally got my brief visits, they were food to my soul. I loved and adored her. Her smile and laugh were the same, and her adoration for me remained. She was my baby, my precious Audra Starr.

As life ebbed on, Audra continued to be a part of my life through my marriages, the birth of my sons, and the coming of my beloved daughter, Hillary. As I moved away from home, my career taking me states away, I began taking calls from my mother, in need of help, Audra was in crisis, she had developed a drug addiction. I would be called numerous times and would make countless trips home over the coming years. I studied the drug of her choice and sought out the best treatment facilities here in the U.S. I knew that Audra was a dual diagnosis patient, this made her treatment complex. The calls and Audra's treatment went on for years.

Left: Precious visit with my baby sister, Audra Starr

I believed Audra was doing well, however, heartbreak was soon to follow. I was called one day to attend the funeral of my grandmother, Ruby. This was a command performance. I knew I'd be seeing my sister, my mother, and extended family, as well as Ahlab and her family, once I arrived back home in Illinois.

I booked flights for Hillary and myself, added a few days in Chicago for some playtime, and off we went. Little did I know what a tragic trip this would turn out to be. Once in Rockford, we dined out with my mother. Audra entered the restaurant, all five-feet-ten-inch of her. She was a shell of herself. Missing teeth, eyes hollow and dark. She had obviously fallen back into the depths of drug use. My heart sank. I turned to my mother and asked, why, how?

We attended my grandmother's funeral and proceeded to Chicago. I booked a suite at the new Hard Rock Hotel. Hillary and I spent our first-day shopping at the Magnificent Mile, one of my favorite shopping venues in Chicago. We spent our evening people-watching from the bar seats at the Hard Rock. Played a fun game of attempting to decide their career choice by the fashion of each individual who walked the sidewalk in front of us. During our first night's stay, Audra rang me and said, "Sissy, I need help." I immediately hired a driver to drive the two-plus hours to pick her up, booked a second room for her to stay near ours, and awaited her arrival. As fate would have it, the driver was a former addict. Audra was in good hands.

As I awaited the arrival of Audra and the driver, I was on pins and needles. Was she going to make it? If so, what was I in for?

Audra arrived late that night. She shared with me that the driver I had hired was wearing an N.A. ring. That presented the opportunity for the two of them to fall into easy conversation regarding drug use and recovery. What a blessing! Nothing is by coincidence; the Gods had placed my sister in just the right hands at just the right time.

Audra may have had her bouts of addiction, yet, when she was clean, she was a giver, she was an active part of N.A., sponsoring many addicts. She helped so many people in their dark days. I know that she was a part of cleaning up the lives of many, she was a “giver”, always’ kind and loving. Then, she would herself fall into the deep, dark despair of addiction.

I spent some time getting her settled in her room, ordered some room service for her, and waited as she showered. Handing her one of the hotel robes, which seemed to swallow her emaciated body. I encouraged her to eat; it was easy to see that she'd not eaten in quite some time. It was painful to watch; my heart was breaking. Each forkful of food seemed an effort. Saying goodnight, I kissed her sweetly, and I can still remember hearing her say... "Thank you, Sissy... I love you..."

The next morning, I was in my robe when I went next door to her room and found her still sleeping. I laid out her clothing and helped her dress. She handed me a small metal box. I was at a loss. What was it, I asked. She explained that I'd need to dispose of it. Out in the hall, I looked in the box and found crack cocaine wrapped in plastic and a pipe. I panicked. I looked up at the security cameras. Here I was, in my robe, at a high-end hotel disposing of illegal drugs. What was I to do! To make matters worse, I had left my daughter alone in our suite next door. I literally shuffled over towards the trash receptacle while keeping one eye on the elevator and the other on the camera. All this time, I prayed my fingerprints were not on that small metal box!

I had called ahead to American Airlines to book a seat for Audra. Hillary and I were flying first class, and luckily, they had an extra seat in the row behind us. Audra was in bad shape. She began having D.T.s in the airport, so I gave her some lorazepam I had on hand, which helped a bit. As we sat waiting at O'Hare airport, I prayed we'd board soon. Soon could not come soon enough.

Once on board the plane, I settled Audra into her seat. The first class was full. Hillary did what she always does on a flight; she pulled out her book of renaissance art and scanned through the pages. We did our fair share of traveling, and for this, I was grateful. I was plenty busy checking on Audra. She was in and out. Without going into any detail, it was a rough flight.

Once we landed, Hillary and I gathered our belongings and prepared to disembark. The gentleman seated directly across from me jumped up and attempted to cross in front of my sister. I threw my leg in front of him and shouted, "YO.! Ladies first," and helped my sister out of her seat and to her feet, which was no easy feat. All of the first class clapped. That man was an ass.

Years later, Audra was clean, raising her son and daughter, my mother was battling cancer for the sixth time, pancreatic cancer. I had asked Audra if she could possibly move in with Mom and help out due to the fact that her husband was also dealing with his second bout of bladder cancer. She made the move, taking her toddler, Trynattee (Tryn), with her. Just months into her stay, she called me, a phone call that I'll never forget. And her next words to me were..."Sissy, I have cancer." Words, etched upon my soul.

Just a few years later, when the end was near, she would ask me to look after her young daughter, Trynattee. I promised her that I would always, for the rest of my days, care for her treasured child. A promise I meant to keep. She did one more thing in those final days, she married the love of her life, Rick, the only father figure her daughter, Trynn, had ever known. Audra felt that by doing so, she was ensuring that Trynn would remain with Rick in his custody. She was wrong.

Above: Audra with her husband, Rick

Upon my sister's death, Tynattee was spirited away by her sister, Alyssa, Audra's eldest daughter, a heroin addict. I, quite honestly, never had much use of this girl. Grief swept over my body and soul. There was not one thing I could do. She had removed Trynn from the advanced school she was attending and the home she knew. Rick, her stepfather, was not allowed to see her. I maintained contact in an effort to keep the waters calm and know the whereabouts of Trynn, and I waited. I waited for Alyssa to overdose. It took two years, and when it happened, I was the first to know. I was on a plane immediately, heading to Illinois. By the time I arrived, the State of Illinois had acquired custody of Trynn and had placed her in foster care. I, as the closest living relative, would be given custody of Trynn. My cousin Ahlab and I made the journey to Rockford, Illinois, and met with Child Protective Services.

It was at this point that Ahlab proposed taking custody of Trynn. She, after all, had her master's in education, and her two children were close in age to Trynn. She promised that Trynn would be allowed to see her stepfather, Rick. My sister, Audra, married Rick shortly before she died; it was her dying wish that Trynattee be raised by Rick. Rick had been in Trynn's life since she was an infant. He was a good man. Ahlab went on to say that Trynn could also maintain contact with her brother, Phalen. What she proposed all made good sense. After all, I was a widow, living on a ranch in Texas. An author and public speaker who spent a great deal of time traveling. I'd have to enroll Trynattee in a prep school an hour plus away, the same prep school, TMI, that my boys attended. She would probably need to be in boarding school during the school year. I'd take Trynn on the road with me during the summer months. I could go either way with this decision. Yet, Ahlab was quite convincing. She has a way of making you see things her way; she has always been a charmer. This little cousin of mine.

So, in the end, I acquiesced. I informed the officials at the State of Illinois that I felt the best place for Trynn was with my cousin, Ahlab. From that point forward, Ahlab took full control and made all the necessary arrangements. She eventually adopted Trynn. Trynn never saw her stepfather Rick or her friends again, and communication with her brother was nearly nonexistent. The saddest thing, the most disgusting thing, was that Ahlab told Trynn repeatedly that her mother, my baby sister Audra, had died of her use of drugs, not of cancer. Let me set the record straight. My sister, Audra, died of neuroendocrine cancer; the fact that she had been a drug user in the past had nothing to do with her death. She was clean for years at the time of her death. I loved my sister. She was my baby, my life, and my love.

I wasn't allowed to travel to Audra's funeral; my doctors denied me this due to it being just months after my brain injury. This just about killed me. I cried for days. I was not there when her precious body was covered head to toe in painful tumors. She was strong until the end. Her last words to me over the phone were..."It's okay, Sissy..." I spoke with my cousin, Ahlab; she lived a short forty minutes from Audra. She had also offered to care for Trynattee following Audra's death. She was aware that Audra had married Rick, her longtime boyfriend, the man who had raised Trynn. It was Audra's wish that Rick raise Audra there in the home that Trynn had been raised in and that she and my mother lived in.

Ahlab agreed to attend the funeral and represent me as best she could. I was to have no worries. This was comforting. I felt a bit better about not being there for Trynn, her brother, and the biggest part, of course, was not being there to say goodbye to my baby, my Audra. I sent a large, lovely assortment of calla lilies to the service with a card that said simply... "Love, Sissy."

Ahlab never attended the funeral, never called Audra's children, and didn't send flowers or a card. She did nothing. She sat forty minutes away and did...... nothing.

Tragically, following my sister's death, her eldest daughter, Alyssa, a heroin addict, physically took Trynn, removing her from the advanced education school she was attending, away from the home she knew and the one person she knew to be a parent figure, Rick, her stepfather. Alyssa literally stole Trynn; she went to court and gained custody of Trynn, collected the social security benefits as both of Trynn's parents were now dead, and dragged Trynn on a drug-induced journey for two years. All I could do was wait. During this time, I spoke with my cousin. Ahlab was unwilling to intervene; she was too busy with her own life to attempt any type of rescue. I was devastated. So, I waited, knowing that at some point, Alyssa would probably mess up or worse, she would overdose, and overdose she did. She overdosed on heroin, not once, but twice in front of my niece. The second time was the last. I was the first to hear of this, and I was on a flight immediately bound for Illinois. I was the closest blood relative, and I was going to make sure that Trynn was placed exactly where my sister wished her to be.

I arrived at Chicago O'Hare airport. Ahlab picked me up, and we made a beeline to Rockford, Illinois. The State of Illinois responded quickly; they had already placed her into the State's protective custody. I would need to jump through this hurdle, gain custody, and then transfer that custody. Ahlab and I met with state officials. When I voiced my sister's last wishes that

Trynn be placed with her stepfather, I was given a setback. The answer was no. He was not a blood relative. I was at a loss; the State was looking to me to take custody. I lived on a ranch in Texas alone; at the time, I was running the Moonlight Fund, had authored two books, and was accepting public speaking engagements. The closest prep school was TMI, the same school my boys had attended. It's a good hour away, and with my travel schedule, well, Trynn would need to board during the school year. I mulled all this over in my mind.

I asked if we might pay a visit to Trynn; she was staying with the grandparents of her half-brother. We were granted a visit. Ahlab and I made our way home and spent more than two hours with Trynn, her brother, and the grandparents. They made it clear that caring for Trynn was a hardship. This broke my heart, I wanted to take her with me right then and there, provide her with a loving home, yet I could do nothing. This presented a more complex situation for me, and my mind reeled. I needed to work through the paperwork the State presented, find the best home for Trynn, and get her placed in that home as soon as possible. There was a reason I purchased a one-way ticket. As I sat in Ahlab's car, driving back to her home in Round Lake Heights, she proposed taking Trynn into her household. She reminded me that at one point, my sister had mentioned her as a possible guardian for Trynn. She went on to say that not only did she have her master's in education, but she also had two children close in age to Trynn. To comfort me further, she assured me that Trynn would be allowed to see her brother and allowed visits with Rick and her friends in Rockford. It seemed like the best choice at the time.

The next day, I rang the officials we had met with at the State of Illinois and shared with them that it was my opinion that

Trynn be placed with Rick, her stepfather. However convincing Ahlab had been, I still felt the best place for Trynn was with her stepfather, Rick. They would not agree to this due to him not being a blood relative, so I gave them my second choice, that of her second cousin, Ahlab Dibbern, in Round Lake Heights, Illinois. They stated they would get back to me with a decision. I had set the wheels in motion, and eventually, Trynn was transferred into the custody of Ahlab. I didn't know it at the time, but I had just sealed the fate of this beautiful young child and had broken the promise I had made to my sister. My decision destined the future of this beautiful young girl.

Trynn never saw her stepfather Rick or her friends during her time in Ahlabs custody. She visited her brother, Phalen, only once. Her life would become a living nightmare. I flew Ahlab, her children and Trynn to Texas on numerous occasions, I also visited Illinois. I began to develop a sense that Ahlab treated Tyrnn with scorn and I made every attempt to intervene and bring out the goodness in Ahlab and remind her of the kindness shown to her by my sister. There were other clues, things that only now, I see, things I should have seen then, things I will always regret.

Mon Coeur

My dogs had been missing since November 6th, 2022. I made a police report with the Boerne police department, which I later found out was closed. I hired one of the top investigative firms here in the U.S. They also do extensive work overseas and have a proven track record of success. If anyone can go into another country and bring back a missing child, they could certainly find my dog. I spent thousands of dollars and countless hours searching for my baby. They first focused their attention on the home of Trish's mother. Her residence was in Sierra Vista, Arizona, near the Mexico border. We were told that she had Risqué. After days of surveillance, including video footage from drones, we were left with no signs of a dog. Not a bowl, a toy, or visible signs of my girl. The team then traveled to Washington state to place surveillance on Trish's home. They confirmed that Taboo was there; however, there were no signs of Risqué. Teams were also sent to Illinois and Texas. The homes of my cousin, Ahlab, in Illinois, and Tubbs, in Boerne, Texas, were also watched and photographed, but still no sign of Risqué.

I made a desperate plea via Facebook. I received support from DAR Members, the airshow community, military members, burn survivors, and friends. Please help me find my dogs and help me bring them home. I registered Risqué's chip and tattoo with numerous nationwide databases. Posts regarding the dogs were circulated nationwide, and my Facebook account was quite busy. Unbeknownst to me, Ahlab had gained access to all my public and private Facebook pages, including Metta Suites, and was posting fake posts on my pages. Several of my friends saw the activity on my accounts and called her out; they also contacted Facebook. I must give much credit to the folks at

Facebook; they were already on the case and watching every move Ahlab made. They also identified several fake Celia Belt pages that were set up by someone we believe to be Adder, the attorney's partner. With this knowledge, we sat back and waited for Ahlab to hang herself. Ahlab's continued fake and negative posts, some targeting the Moonlight Fund, were all documented for future use. I vowed to never stop looking for my baby, Risqué. I was determined to bring her home.

Above: With my beloved girl, I will never give up hope of finding her.

Ahlab gave up her job quite some time back. It's obvious that she has way too much time on her hands; she must spend hours hacking into other people's accounts, planning and plotting ways to seize the assets of others, and, quite simply, being slovenly lazy. The filth she left behind in my home is evident of her lifestyle. In the initial report prepared by my investigators, they found that both Ahlab and Tubbs had multiple bankruptcies, foreclosures, and failed businesses. The two of them were looking for an easy target, and it was me. I opened the door and gave Ahlab a lot of information. I took her to my bank, she asked to be P.O.D. on all accounts. I shared with her the assets I had, the equity I had in my home, the value of my life insurance policies, and much more. I did this; I was at fault. I had also spoiled Ahlab from the day she was born. My children did all they could to warn me; they were concerned after reading several of her texts demanding large sums of money, new appliances for her home, and trips for her family. Yet, I was oblivious and told them to mind their own business. My constant reply to them was "stay in your own lane". How dare they call into question the love I bore for my younger cousin and that she bore me? I was, plainly put, stupid.

I trusted Ahlab. I took her to one of my banks at her request. I drew out large sums of cash at her request, never thinking that was out of the ordinary. She also asked to be put on as POD on several accounts, and I complied. She, Ahlab, was family, and I had vowed, since the death of my baby sister, Audra, that I would always care for her daughter, Trynn, a girl now firmly in the custody of Ahlab. In my mind, taking care of Ahlab, I was also keeping the promise to my sister. Right? I was also continuing to spoil Ahlab, just as I had for so many years.

She knew that I had a great deal of equity in my home, that I owed nothing on my furnishings or car, that my liquid assets were substantial, and that the lines of credit on my cards were high and had been paid in full monthly. She also knew that I had two large life insurance policies and that my art collection was of high value. She had also contacted my brother and was colluding with him in regards to gaining access to my mother's annuity. I was the perfect target, a widow, no longer cared for by a protective husband, a woman with a brain injury, and numerous health issues. I had a target on my back, I was baited, and I fell for it. Hook, line, and sinker.

Once I knew what was going on and who the players were, I set about the task of protecting myself. My credit cards had been maxed, the money in the bank had been compromised, and I had very little left. My credit score tanked from nearly 800 to 400. The one thing she, her conspirators, and the workers in the psych units couldn't take away from me was my faith. My dignity was battered, I will admit. There were many times while I was incarcerated in psych units that I cried up to the Gods. "What have I done to deserve such treatment?" I had to remind myself that Jesus suffered more and that somehow, in some way, I would get through this terrible trial. Would I survive? Could I survive? I honestly didn't know.

I saw things, unspeakable, terrible things done to people in those places. I made a promise to those people that one day, I would use this voice of mine. I would speak of their pain, their suffering. Their cries will not go unheard. If I ever got out, those cries would find a voice, my voice. They may be gone, but my voice would carry their suffering forward, and the message would be heard for all to hear. This type of inhumane treatment, families locking up their loved ones, and a society that condones and builds such facilities is abominable. I will speak on this and many other topics. I will be a voice for all those voices that have faded, long gone, and since forgotten. Do we call our society civilized? Are we in the times of Constantinople? When slavery is condoned?

I speak about forgiveness in my first book, Remarkably Intact. Several of my quotes are regarding forgiveness and just how empowering this simple act can be. I can and will forgive all those who took so much from me, yet I will not forget. I will never stop searching for Risqué and have every intention of bringing my baby back to Texas. Her home is with me. I imported both dogs at the age of four months. I am and will always be their "mother." The memories of traveling to the Houston airport and picking them up are embedded in my mind and my soul. The joy they brought me cannot be measured in words. For those of you who have a beloved animal in your life, I would say this, treasure every moment. Every ball tossed, every greeting bark, and the feel of that fur. I never dreamed that someone would take my dog; it is unthinkable, and it is unimaginable. One day you are walking freely with them by your side, enjoying their companionship and delighting in their attention, when the next they are gone. I live each day wondering if Risqué is well-treated and well-loved. Is she cold, hungry, or just confused? I also think of Taboo. Although I know where he is, I wonder if he forgives me and if I'll ever see him again. I hope he brings as much joy to his new owners as he brought me.

Members of the Daughters of The American Revolution awarded me the Distinguished Citizen Medal back in 2018. An honor I will never forget. As I accepted that award, just months after Randy's death, my first public speaking event since having lost him, I threw my notes to the side and spoke from my heart. These million-strong memberships once again came together to help me find my dog. I had one of the best private investigation companies money could buy, my DAR members, airshow contacts, Facebook friends, and followers. My dog has a tattoo and a chip.. Yet, we are at a loss as to what they did with my cherished Risqué. She was such a loving and sweet dog, and the thought of not knowing where she is ...is more than I can bear. I spent countless nights screaming in my bedroom, they took my babies!!!

In November, I fully realized the extent of what had been stolen from me, not just my dog but also my valuables, but my identity. My social security card, credit card, and bank account information had been compromised, as had all my social media sites. My identity had been stolen. Cutting my hair off, that was just one way of separating myself from their destruction, there was no true way of separating myself from their intent. They would continue in their efforts to destroy me, my good name and seek my assets. How can anyone be so heartless, so cruel and so full of hate. It is beyond me.

During the previous summer, 2022, I brought Ahlab, her two children, and my niece down to Texas from Illinois for a bit of R and R. I also invited Tubbs' son down; at the time, he had struck up a relationship with Ahlab's daughter. I planned for them to spend a week at my home in Boerne and another week at a home I had rented at the beach down on the Texas coast.

I went all out. Spending in excess of ten thousand dollars on a luxury home on the beach. Everyone had their own room. This did not, however, stop Ahlab's daughter and Tubbs' son from spending the nights together, something I had hoped to avoid. I understand young love; I also understand that they need to play by my rules, and those rules are not sleeping around, especially with younger children in the home. My niece and my grandson were present. As were my daughter and Ahlab's son. Things became complicated. I found myself playing a police officer at night, monitoring the hallways to keep this Romeo and

Juliet apart. In the end, my efforts failed. They were openly sleeping together, due in part to Ahlab and Tubbs, both parents, condoning such behavior. I simply had to give in and give up. I turned the other cheek and focused my time on my grandson and daughter. My daughter had arranged for her photographer to pay a visit and photograph our group. Ahlab would have some lovely, professional photos of her family. I paid the photographer and told Ahlab to choose whatever photos she liked. The week was perfect. The beach, wind, and sun agreed in perfect harmony.

It was during this trip that Ahlab would take numerous photographs of my home, later posting them on her Facebook page. These photos would be telling clues later. She never included me in any of the photos, she presented these photos as if this were her home. She featured her daughter in the photos, showcasing my staircase, kitchen, pool, fireplace, my art collection and several features of the home. Once again, she was claiming my life as her own.

At night, I'd stay up late with Ahlab, listening to her talk. I'd drink wine, and I was always careful to drink a glass of water in between each glass of wine. Ahlab drank the beer I purchased for her, one after another. She many times got drunk and would go on the attack, most times towards her son. She would say the meanest things to him. Accusing him of being just like his father. I could not believe my ears. His father had committed suicide only two years before. What a ghastly thing to say, yet here she was, three sheets to the wind, yelling at her young son, "You're just like your father!" I watched as this young boy cringed. You could almost see him become a part of the sofa. She didn't stop there.

She went on to call him a liar and a thief and to tell him he'd amount to nothing. At one point, she grabbed my wallet and accused him of stealing. I told her I had previously removed the cash, she would not hear of it, and continued to rail against her son, accusing him of stealing from my wallet; it was more than I could bear. I wanted to turn to her and say, "Stop!" but I couldn't. Fact is, I was afraid of her; she was three, perhaps, four times my size and she was mighty drunk. Not the person you want to piss off. So, I did nothing, and to this day, I regret that. For, in the years to come, that same young boy would sexually assault my niece. I wonder if the abuse from his mother had anything to do with his inclination to do such horrific things to my niece. I live with this thought.

As the night progressed, Ahlab went into a rage; she began speaking about her childhood in a way I had never heard before. I adored her parents, my aunt and uncle. Her parents meant the world to me, and suddenly, I was hearing things about them that would make my world turn upside down. I knew she needed to talk, and I had to listen. She was, after all, my beloved younger cousin. She went into great detail, telling me how she had been mistreated as a child and belittled due to her sex. How her two brothers were always favored in the eyes of her father, and how good was never good enough. She went on to say how her mother had become compliant with all her father was doing and did not stand for the rights that she felt she deserved as a female. This was not the aunt I knew. The strong band director that nearly kicked my ass across the band room all those years ago, the woman I knew was not the woman she was describing. No, I had to listen, but I would not believe her words.

I was beginning to realize that Ahlab had such deep-seated resentment that nothing I said or did would come close to healing her. All I could do was listen. There were things she said that I cannot share in this book because I could not or would not believe them to be true. Grotesque abuse at the hands of her parents and siblings. It may have been the alcohol talking, for all I know. Who knows what was real or what was the alcohol talking? She talked into the wee hours, describing her teen years, how she had become sexually promiscuous due to the abuse at home, and had started abusing alcohol due to this abuse. She was searching for approval and found it in the arms of those she found in bars.

She also touched on an episode that happened in 2014, just briefly; she mentioned that she was charged with assaulting an eighteen-year-old boy, then went on to say it was all fake. That was all she was willing to say. I found this to be alarming, as it was the first time I had heard of it. My heart broke for her as I listened. I had never heard all of this, and I was shocked. I was in disbelief, and I didn't know what to say. Perhaps this is why she treated her son with such disdain and abuse. She thought nothing of telling him he was just like his late father; she also physically abused him in front of other people. Perhaps this is why she left her first husband when he had a brain injury... She left him...alone in assisted living? She also sent her second husband away for treatment and did not allow him to see his children once he completed his treatment, a cruel thing to do. Was this to blame? I don't know, it was all very heavy. She went on to share that she got her master's degree in teaching not so much to get her degree but as a way to "one up" her parents. Neither of her parents had their masters, and she felt by getting hers, she was making a strong point.

As I listened, I became afraid, afraid of this person. This was not the person I had nearly raised. The person I had known since infancy. The younger cousin I adored, this was a vengeful, self-seeking, hateful person out for revenge. Everything she was sharing with me, every person she mentioned, had a target on their back. She began speaking about her sister-in-law, Samatha. I listened, and then sheer terror set in. I remembered that her brother, Nick and his wife and their young children had lived with Ahlab and she had kicked them out, the details were never shared with me. I could not believe what I was hearing. These were people that she should have loved; these were family members. I was raised to love family, and here she was, speaking with such malice and hate about her own family.

It was almost too much. I was becoming more frightened by the moment. As she went into great detail about each and every person in her life she felt had wronged her and her plans for them, I was speechless. I spoke to her about forgiveness. My words fell on deaf ears. Her body language was frightening me, her eyes full of rage, her words slurred, due in part to drinking, yes, but also to something more sinister. There was something evil, something very dark, taking place right before my eyes. I was thankful that I had mixed my wine with water; my mind was clear, and I was taking in all that she said. I sat there for hours, I watched, I listened and I began to fear this person, somewhere deep down inside me, she intimidated me on a level I can't quite describe.

When she finally climbed the stairs to bed, I retired to my bedroom on the first floor, locking the door. I lay there for hours, unable to sleep, my mind full of what had just occurred. Had I just heard all she had just said? Was this real? Would she remember, or was it just the alcohol talking. Regardless, I got little sleep. The next day, I prepared a late lunch and sat and waited as Ahlab came down the stairs, late in the afternoon, acting as if nothing had occurred the night before, I was almost thankful for her loss of memory.

My mind also went to Aunt Dianne. For years, Ahlab constantly would say, "When Aunt Dianne dies." I thought nothing of it. Hearing these words became second nature. Now, it has become something very dark. I realized she had been playing Aunt Dianne for years, posturing herself as the poor little niece part, playing on her sympathies, assuming she'd get a payout in the end. Ahlab even brought one of Aunt Dianne's patents back to the U.S. and pretended to market it. What she did was take as much money as was possible and then bankrupted it. (This last piece of information was shared with me by my private investigators.) This was just sick on an entirely new level. Stealing from a family member. I could only hope that my cousins saw through this charade. We had a wolf in the den.

Misunderstanding

In regards to brain injuries and those suffering seizures, there's so much negative misunderstanding out there, and I know I speak for many who suffer from traumatic brain injuries. The seizures, vertigo, and memory loss can be maddening. The fear of having a seizure in public is constant. During the war, people were more tolerant; now, people tend to be less knowledgeable. The police force is younger and less educated, and they have not seen active duty. Those of us who have, or who have been exposed to, those who have experienced a TBI are the only ones who can truly grasp the enormity of the situation. It's so demoralizing to be in the throes of a full-blown seizure and have law enforcement looking on, telling you ... that you are faking it. While you are begging your body to come out of it. It's an indescribable terror. Something I hope I never hope to live through again. Yet, I lived through it more than once. Perhaps there was a reason, and perhaps that reason was there needed to be a voice. I did, after all, have tens of thousands of followers around the world. I could be a voice for all those unheard. My other pet projects, and those for which I will continue to raise funding, are as follows: burn survivors, traumatic brain injuries, college funds for girls, third-world issues, the abuse of narcotic pain prescriptions and so much more. Civil rights and amendment rights.

I purchased Taboo the year before my riding accident. I completed his obedience training quickly, and he was my constant companion. In the summer of 2017, I suffered a subarachnoid hematoma. I also ruptured my inner vestibular in the accident. In layman's terms, I have a traumatic brain injury. Three lobes of my brain were badly damaged, and I lost the hearing out of my left ear and suffered from near-constant vertigo. I wrote my second book on this experience. I at first did not want to admit I had such an injury; after all, I was trained to deal with TBIs, and many of the patients I cared for through my work with burn injuries had secondary injuries, those injuries included TBIs. I could not and would not accept that I had a TBI. I was in deep denial. All the testing in the world could not convince me otherwise.

Left: Pondering my future

When Randy and I knew his end was near, we spoke of my collecting widow's benefits from Social Security. Once we looked into this, we discovered that I did not qualify due to my age. I was fifty-five, too young to collect these benefits unless I was also collecting disability. I flatly refused. I was too proud to collect disability. I would not hear of it. Yet, you cannot collect widows' benefits without being on disability. I was up against the wall this time. All I wanted to do was spend time with him, I didn't want to think about the future, about finances. Sunsets without him, days spent without that voice, his guiding words. To say nothing of his body wrapped around mine, missing that. Nothing mattered to me, nothing but him. My heart was breaking, my world ending, the colors of my life were fading.

Randy and I spent his last days filled with laughter and love. Memories of our hunting trips, the times we spent, covered in blood from our kills, only to make love on the open ground filled the days. We never stopped kissing. He wanted to cross over at our ranch, so we made arrangements for a private jet to bring him home to Texas. There we spent those last two weeks, surrounded by the Texas hill country and our animals at the ranch we both loved. Our friend, Mark, spent one week with the two of us, I know that meant so much to Randy. When he did cross over, Bethany was at my side, and it was beautiful. I lay there, on top of him, for two hours, I felt the life here, this life, leave him, as he entered the next. My beautiful, powerful, guiding man, the one I cherished above all others. When they came to take him, Bethany had to restrain me in another room, I just could not let them take him, not my Randy. I watched as they lovingly wrapped his body in white sheets. The body I had made love to for these past ten years, the strong body that had held me close, hunted by my side, kept me safe, and offered me more than one firm scolding on several occasions. Then, he was gone. The house grew quiet and still, the fire burned and I stared into it for hours, a piece of my heart left me, and will forever be with him.

Throughout history, brain injuries and epilepsy have been misdiagnosed and misunderstood. The great Roman dictator, Julius Caesar, exhibited signs of epilepsy shortly after becoming a dictator. After years spent on the battlefield, having sustained numerous injuries and perhaps head injuries, he was left with a debilitating condition that appeared to be epileptic seizures. At the time, this was viewed as a weakness in a leader, something deeming him unfit to rule. His enemies, many of whom were in the senate, saw this as a means to eliminate him and plotted against him with no luck. He continued to rule, pass laws, and fight for the freedoms of his people. In the end, he was murdered by senate members, stabbed 23 times. He was a genius, a leader, in spite of his medical frailties.

Alexander the Great died at age thirty-three. The greatest leader and conquer of all time, suffered after years of grueling battles; he was said to have had the "falling sickness", which was thought of as a sacred disease. This belief stemmed from the thought that those with seizures were either possessed by the evil spirits or touched by the Gods. I ask you, does this type of ignorance still exist today, and are we still living in the dark ages, where we condemn those that are suffering?

The Bodyguard

I felt very unsafe and in need of protection, so I hired a bodyguard. My home had been looted, my computer had been hacked, my safe broken into, and personal files rummaged through. Photos used for lewd purposes and so much more, I felt so unsafe. Police were constantly at my door or searching my home. Life had reached a new level of complete madness. I'd met Kodey on three occasions. We simply kept crossing paths, and I felt a need to chat with him. He appeared to be quite intelligent and superbly confident. He was extremely tall and athletic and spoke fluent Arabic. During our third chat, I asked him if he had his class 4 (basically asking him if he was licensed to carry numerous different types of firearms). He responded by stating he had his class 3. I also asked if he had ever provided any private security and if it was something he'd be interested in doing. As our conversation progressed, I knew that I wanted this young man on my team. I was afraid I'd been through hell, and I did not want to carry a firearm on my person. I was feeling extraordinarily vulnerable.

We exchanged numbers, and I said I'd be in touch. The next day, I gave him a ring, and he had already begun the process of applying for his class 4. I was impressed. I am a young person with a work ethic, and now there's something I can respect. We met later that day, and he was hired. He was such a help to me in so many ways. He took over the responsibilities of dealing with the credit card company and my identity theft situation. He also helped organize every aspect of my life. I hired him to make me feel safe; what I got was a full-blown personal assistant and a dynamite bodyguard. I tend to be overly friendly out in public, something I've learned I should be cautious of. When Randy was alive, he protected me in ways I never saw, much like Kevin Costner in the movie *The Bodyguard*. I was much like Whitney Houston. I always put myself out there, always in the public eye, and always trust the wrong people. With Randy gone, I was exposed, I was helpless, and I didn't know it. Kodey helped curb that; he also never took his eyes off me and anyone who was looking my way. I felt safe. I hadn't had a night's sleep in months. Most nights, I'd sleep for an hour or two and wake up with the pillows soaked with sweat and terrible terrors. Just days after hiring him, I slept, and when I woke up, the sheets were dry.

Left: I always value a good cigar.

Shortly after hiring Kodey, I saw a post on Facebook. I knew at this point that Taboo was being held in Washington. The dog in the post was a female who had been hit by a car and had obviously shaved off her beautiful long coat. She was lying in a cage that looked like something out of a third world. It appeared to be my girl, Risqué. It was a heart-wrenching site to take in. We began work on tracking down who had made the post. I also contacted one of my contacts, Darlene Montgomery, a DAR member in the Seattle area. I looked into flights, and there was nothing available on such short notice, so I rented a car, quickly packed, and off we went. We estimated a three-day journey to get from Boerne, Texas, to Seattle, Washington. I was grateful that I had Kodey with me to do all the driving, as I had not yet taken up driving since my accident.

The drive was good for my soul. After months of torment, hospitalizations, and theft of my property and person, I was able to let my hair down and just be me. I took in the stunning scenery, the mountains, the blue sky, and the cities as we made our journey. Every convenience store we stopped at was like Christmas to me. I found so many wonderful gifts and mementos to bring back to family and friends, unique items that you simply don't find in Texas. We also stopped by a few dispensaries. I had never been to one. I don't smoke; I do, however, know of people who do. Once again, there were Christmas gifts to be found at each stop. At some point, I believe we were in New Mexico or perhaps Arizona, I was offered a cannabis gummy and it was explained to me that it was legal in that area. I believe we crossed three states before I stopped laughing. It's a true story! What a journey we had.

Although this was an emotional trip to make, we had so much damn fun! We also encountered our fair share of challenges. Our first stop was in Alpine, Texas. I really wanted to show Kodey the Marfa lights, an experience everyone should embrace. I had some difficulty finding lodging on such short notice. I finally found a room at the Big Bend Biker Hotel. It was a long nine-hour drive to Alpine, Texas, and I was relieved to see that the bar was still open. We found a seat, met the couple seated next to us, and made small talk with the bartender.

When it was time to grab our bags and head to the room, things went south and quickly. I had another grand-mal seizure in front of the hotel. As I was lying on the ground, my body shaking and unable to talk, I looked up at Kodey and saw such empathy in his eyes. I also saw fear. I was attempting to say, "Don't call 911." All I could get out was utterances. The owners of the hotel had arrived, and soon after, an EMS crew was on site. They were preparing to load me up when the seizure started to subside, and I could speak. I flatly refused. I would not allow the EMS crew to take me again, not after what happened to me back in October. The two firemen were extremely kind, understanding, and persuasive, yet I stood firm. Once I regrouped, I felt comfortable putting the owners of the hotel at ease. They had just witnessed a horrific sight, a woman flailing about, peeing her pants, and farting, as Kodey would later tell me. I suggested we move on and find another place to stay. Kodey agreed. Once in the car, he began looking for anything available. Finally, our luck changed, and he came across a dump of a motel that had a room. We were both exhausted, physically and emotionally; we'd have slept in a ditch. Our luck didn't hold out. Once we checked in, I had another seizure. As Kodey clutched me in his arms, a look of sheer terror in his eyes, I saw him dial 911.

The same two paramedics arrived. This time, they explained that legally, they would be required to take me to an emergency room. I was loaded into the ambulance with Kodey following close behind. Once I was settled in my room and the initial vitals and medical history were conducted, the staff simply disappeared. I explained to them that I had seizure disorder due to a traumatic brain injury and that I simply needed to get back to the hotel, take my anti-seizure meds, and rest. I began to feel extremely uncomfortable with the situation. I got out of bed, grabbed my things, and walked to the nurse's station. Once again, I explained my need for rest and that I was not in need of emergency medical care. I was told that I could not leave the hospital under any circumstances. My response to that was, "Watch me!" I walked out those sliding doors, Kodey by my side, and we resumed our journey. There would be no sleep that night, just a long stretch of road they call I-10 in Texas.

Our next stop was in Clint, Texas, with a population of nine hundred and twenty-six. Kodey called ahead and found us a place; they only had one room available. That truly didn't matter to me. I trusted him with my life. I think I could trust him to sleep in the same room. As it turned out, I had stayed at the very same hotel as a young girl with my grandmother, Iris. She was killed at age fifty-four in a head-on collision with a semi-truck. A striking beauty and a woman full of adventure. I will never forget the summer she took me across the country, stopping to look at a horse for sale here and there and buying me precious gifts. I adored her. I lost her when I was in the third grade. It was eerie being back at the same hotel. I remembered the entire layout, the little diner out front, the parking in front of each room. Kodey was dead on his feet; he quickly took some time to pray. Carefully folding and laying his blanket at his feet, I respected his faith. I watched him kneel on his mat and distantly observed a man who had just spent countless hours driving and had gone without sleep for a day. My respect for him was growing. I hope he knew that.

As it turned out, I didn't sleep at all that night. I had, once again, gone days without sleep. I sat outside the room, looking at the latest copy of Life magazine, had a glass of wine, and smoked a cigar. When I caught my first glimpse of the sunrise, I was anxious to get back on the road and make it to Washington as soon as possible. I kept my enthusiasm in check and remembered that this man was just thirty years of age. He needed this sleep, and we had quite a long journey ahead of us. I made my way to the diner, ordered breakfast, and had a quick conversation with the folks at adjoining tables. The place hadn't changed. It was all as I had remembered it, from my childhood, when I had been here with my grandmother. I took in the sights, the smells, and the sounds of the room. I simply enjoyed each and every moment of it. I was in no hurry to get back to the room. I'd let Kodey sleep for a while. I had found my own dream right here in this little diner on the edge of Texas.

We made it to Utah. Exhaustion fueled our laughter, and we somehow managed to keep pushing forward. Then, tragedy and heartache struck. We discovered that the post with the female German Shepherd, the dog we were driving across the country to retrieve, was fake. I had already reconciled myself to the fact that it might not be Risqué. Regardless, that dog needed a rescue. Kodey made good use of the turbocharged Toyota, spinning it around in the middle of the highway. I was furious with him. He was taking my life in his hands; he might also attract the attention of the police. With firearms in the car, I was understandably concerned. I had to get a little firm with him at this point, reminding him who he worked for and that my life was not to be put at risk. I hated to be that way; it was, nevertheless, necessary.

As we made our way into New Mexico, I stated that I'd like to stop in Santa Fe. My "playground" is what I have so often called it. I always stay at the St. Francis, and I dine at the Coyote Café. I wanted to share some of that fun with Kodey; he deserved it after having driven so far and for so long. He flatly refused. Stating that we needed to get home, resume the search for the dogs, and get back to business. Well, this is where the fight began. You see, he was behind the wheel, unwilling to take the exit for Santa Fe, while I was in the passenger seat, making reservations and damned determined that was where we were going. Long story short...I won... we went to Santa Fe, stayed at St. Francis, and dined out at Coyote Café'. I even got him his own room, thinking it would be an opportunity for him to rest. We had a lovely time. It was good to see him rested and relaxed. I felt a great deal of gratitude towards him, and this was my small way of showing my appreciation.

We hit the road after our brief stay in Santa Fe. I was a bit heartsick; we had not found Risqué, and I was returning home from all the stress I had left behind. To say nothing of Santa Fe being in the rearview mirror. Regardless, off we went. Once again, I could not get enough convenience store shopping. Each time we stopped for gas, I'd be off shopping. Kodey was a great sport; he not only waited, sometimes hours, as I filled the checkout counter with my finds, but he also packed and repacked the car in an effort to make it all fit. We needed to find a place for a good night's rest on our way through Texas. Van Horn, Texas appeared to be a good stopping point. He had called ahead and booked us two rooms at the Hotel El Capitan. I walked into the lobby and fell in love; it reminded me so much of a place I stayed at in Mexico. The Spanish façade, European tiled floors, and wrought iron staircase called out to me like a siren. I was also happy to hear the nearby laughter exuding from the hotel's pub, the Gopher Hole Bar. We checked in, and I took the short route to the bar.

Once again, I made friends quickly and struck up conversations on both sides of my seat as Kodey patiently watched over me. I met a military veteran who was funny as hell; in fact, I asked if he wouldn't mind if I took a video of him telling one of his amusing stories. A good night's rest was ours to be had, and I found comfort in the lovely accommodations provided to me. I arose early and, as you might have guessed, made my way to the lobby. I could smell the aroma of freshly brewed coffee and help myself to a cup. I took in the amazing iron chandeliers hanging from the fourteen-foot ceilings and the way the dimly lit room cast shadows in all directions. I couldn't help but wonder what history this place must have. I allowed my mind a bit of daydreaming of the people who had walked these floors before me. Built in 1930, it is known as one of the "gateway hotels" and is on the edge of Big Bend. This place surely must have been the home of many interesting travelers. I must have it on any radar. I found the equitably turned-out gift shop filled with so many distinctive items. Once again, I found myself picking out items for those I loved and secretly wishing I could share this magical place with all of them someday. Hours later, Kodey appeared, packed and ready to go. We said goodbye to Van Horn and hello to the highway. We were on the road again.

We listened to our jams, laughed, and fought over music selections. That's pretty much what you'd expect any two people would do in confined quarters on a long road trip. On the way home, Kodey informed me that we would need to drop back by Clint, Texas. I asked for whatever, but that's out of the way. I knew, however, he must have a good reason, and what a good reason that was! He had left one of his nine-millimeters under his pillow at the hotel we had stayed at days previous. The police had it, and we'd need to stop by the station and pick it up. I got a hoot out of that, my tall, imposing bodyguard walking into a police station. I have the photos to prove it.

When we arrived home, Kodey backed the car in the drive. For the first time, I truly looked at the car; it was packed to the brim with all my "finds" from our trip. Kodey unpacked the car, and I made my way into the house. I caught up with my contractors, inspecting their work. Then, as I was walking outside, something in the yard caught my eye. Something very shiny was lying there, where it shouldn't be, almost calling my name. I walked out into the yard, and, bending over, I discovered a quarter, so silver, it appeared new. Just lying there. Just like so many occasions before, I felt like Randy had sent me a sign, and on this day, he was saying, "Welcome home."

Throughout this ordeal, I have never been truly "alone." Randy constantly sends me signs, a penny here and there, a business card tucked into one of my books, and a spent shell from one of his rifles. The signs are numerous and consistent. The message is the same: hang in there; I'm here. The Gods have never left my side and have kept me alive, and my prayers are feeding my soul. When I was so cold on the units, and hunger was plaguing me, I was sustained by the bread that only the Gods can serve. I am grateful, and I am humble; it was my faith that kept me strong.

Shock

On January 9th, 2023, I was sitting at my computer, chatting with a burn survivor in Pakistan, when suddenly I began having back-to-back grand-mal seizures. I had to let the patient go, and with much struggle, in between seizures, I made an attempt to post to Facebook that I was experiencing bad seizures. The mouse fell to the floor, and so did I. As I flailed about, unable to control my convulsive body, my eyes searched for my phones. I needed help quickly. As one seizure ended, I managed to dial 911. I explained that I was having seizures and could they please take me to Sid Peterson Hospital in Kerrville, Texas. It's the same distance to the San Antonio hospitals, and after my last 911 experience and them placing me in a psych unit, I was not about to allow treatment unless we had an understanding. I was told they would not transport me there. The call ended. I rang them back once again. This time, I was very upset. I could not control the seizures, and the terror was real.

Once again, I pleaded that I would be taken to Kerrville, and once again, the operator told me no. This was not a pleasant call; I was afraid for my life, and I was rude and demanding good care. I suffered through three more back-to-back seizures. At this point, it made no difference where they took me; just please get here quickly and provide some measure of help. Some time passed, and there was a knock on the door. I yelled out, "Just one moment," and opened the door. There I found two Kendall County Sheriffs standing on my porch. The large officer closest to me attempted to lure me out of the house. I knew better than to do this and asked them to state why they were there and what they wanted from me. In an instant, they bolted through the doorway, placed handcuffs tightly behind my back, and dragged me into my living room. I pleaded with them to please tell me what I had done and begged that the handcuffs be loosened. I continued to tell them I had called 911 for help. I was having seizures, and with the handcuffs so tightly fastened behind my back, I could not flail my arms. I could feel the damage beginning in my hands due to the handcuffing and the flailing about when seizing. They stated that I had made abusive calls to 911. I attempted to explain to them why I sounded so agitated on the phone, but they were not interested in anything I had to say.

I asked when the paramedics would arrive and was met with cold stares and disdain. E.M.S. finally arrived on the scene, and a man and woman team arrived. They took my blood pressure, 168, over something. They took it a second time, and it was 154. I told them my blood pressure is quite low, usually 105 over 70. They stood and watched as I once again had a severe seizure. I pleaded with them to please take the cuffs off or at least loosen them. During one seizure, I attempted to speak. I could say very little. I did manage to get the word "Help" out of my mouth. I was terrified. This was perhaps the most disturbing part of the evening, watching two medical professionals stand over me and offer no assistance. They are trained medical professionals, yet they offer no help. The male E.M.S. worker seemed to be concerned, but he deferred to the officers.

I begged him to please remove the cuffs as I felt another seizure coming on. The officers told me I was faking the seizures. I could feel that I had wet my pants. I wish I was faking. Wetting my pants and flailing about in front of three men and one woman is not my idea of fun. E.M.S. workers eventually left the scene, with me still in handcuffs. They left part of their equipment behind—their blood pressure cuff—it serves as a reminder of the night I cried out for help and received none.

They can chain me, they will never break me!

Once the seizures had subsided, I pleaded with both the Sheriff's deputies to please loosen the handcuffs. My pleas went unheard, and the damage done to my hands due to my flailing about during my seizures with super tight handcuffs on behind my back will be with me for a lifetime and was later documented by E.R. testing. My hands will never be the same. I live in pain, and the visible damage is clear for anyone to see. E.M.S. left me there; they watched me suffer and never offered any aid. I think that's what is the most hurtful, that a medical professional would allow such an atrocity to happen on their shift. I've spent years working in the medical community, and I cannot imagine any of those I have known inflicting so much pain and being so neglectful. This was my second experience with Boerne E.M.S. My first, I was put into a psych unit after a seizure, and now my second. Both were uncalled-for acts of pure neglect and disregard for a fellow human being. They received a call, a call for help, and provided nothing but harm.

After the E.M.S. workers left, things became even more complex. The Sheriff's deputies informed me that I was arrested due to my calls to 911. That was the original charge, and then later, I was served with papers that included the names of Ahlab, Tubbs, Trish, and her husband. They were filing charges, stating I had threatened them on Facebook. I thought I was done with them. I have forgiven them in my mind, or at least a part of me did. I would never cast a terroristic threat on the internet or anywhere. I'm smarter than to do such a thing!

When the officers were at my home, the first officer asked if I had any weapons in the house. I said yes. A Glock 9 mil in my back left pocket with an empty magazine, a Toor blade in my back right pocket, and a Marlin Spike in the front right of my cargo pants. I had been opening boxes earlier in the evening and had the items in my pockets. I turned obediently to allow him to remove each. He did so with more might than was necessary. After that, the second officer began tearing apart my kitchen, I assume, to find any ammunition I might have. I don't keep ammunition in the house Due to having a grandson. I only purchased the gun recently after the local police assaulted me in my own home in December and due to Ahlab and her continued threats. I no longer felt safe. Having a gun in my home made me feel safe. This gun never left my home; it was on the property. The fact that I don't keep ammo on hand matters not.

I made a vain attempt to exercise my civil rights, but my argument fell on deaf ears. Both officers dragged me out to the squad vehicle. My legs, badly swollen due to a pulmonary issue, prevented me from walking as fast as they were dragging me. Once outside, I screamed, "HELP! CALL 911!" as loudly as I could. I was desperate, hoping that one of my neighbors might hear my calls for help. At this point, one officer became very agitated; he roughly attempted to cover my mouth. No one came. There was no help. Neighbors either didn't hear my screams or chose to disregard them. I was shoved into the back of the vehicle, still in handcuffs and with swollen legs, feet, and ankles. It was difficult to enter the seat. The officer shoved me in, screaming at me the entire time. Once inside, I was secured, and the door shut.

A better way to put it is...and the truth is...I was dragged to the vehicle, thrown into the back seat, and fastened in. The second officer entered the front seat, and we sat and waited as the first, more abusive of the two, reentered my home. I became very quiet and waited. The first officer was gone for quite some time. I had no idea, why he spent so much time in my home. The second officer finally drove away, taking me to the county jail. As we turned the corner, I saw a second police vehicle; they had been casing the house and arrived only after my bodyguard and my sub-contractors had vacated the property. Was this all set up? Had they been waiting until I was alone?

I was originally told that I was arrested for retaliation. How can you retaliate with handcuffs on behind your back? Certainly, all involved would take a look at the bodycam footage and see the truth. The video would show me having seizures, being grabbed at my front door, handcuffed, dragged through my home, thrown down, and then undergoing more seizures while still in handcuffs; this video would certainly clear matters up, would it not? Then, the next day, as I sat in the holding cell, I was served with papers. Trish, her husband, and Tubbs were accusing me of terroristic threats on my Facebook page. Again, I felt that all anyone had to do was look at the evidence. My page reflected no threat, yet I was about to pay the price of so much confusion. The actual evidence in this case would never be disclosed, and I would later be a victim of much confusion.

Once at the jail, I was subjected to a level of cruelty that I can only describe as inhumane. I was kept in a cold holding cell with nothing but a metal bench, metal commode, and sink. I have Reynaud's disease; it's a circulatory disorder. The cold was painful. I was also denied medication for my seizures and the blood clots in my brain. I was diagnosed with a tennis ball-sized blood clot in my brain in 2021 and have been on Eliquis since that time. Both medications are prescribed twice-a-day doses. I went a total of 46 hours without access to my meds. I could feel onset seizures, to say nothing of the effects of Reynauds; it was terrifying. I was dragged out of the cell, still barely able to walk, numerous times to be fingerprinted. I don't know why they needed multiple fingerprints. Perhaps it was to watch me cry. My hands were badly damaged as a result of being handcuffed behind my back so tightly, and having seizures with handcuffs on was painful. This made it nearly impossible to fingerprint me without acute pain. my fingers were so badly damaged that they could not be bent for the fingerprinting. But endure it, I did.

I pleaded with the officers to allow me to make bail. I had packed a bag just the night before in preparation to enter the hospital and have the necessary procedures to reduce the swelling in my ankles, feet, and legs. Next to my bag, I had four blue banking zippered pouches containing the last of the cash I had hidden in the house. Twenty-six thousand one hundred dollars in one-hundred-dollar bills. I had decided it best to take it with me to the hospital rather than to leave it in the house with contractors actively working. If only they would allow me access to my home, I could grab the cash and make a bond. Or, if they would allow me to call my daughter, she could pick up the cash.

I was refused this right, and my daughter was forced to come up with the money to make bail. She showed up the next day, twenty-eight hours later. She was accompanied by one of my sub-contractors, Jen, a woman who took her own time to come to the jail the previous day in an attempt to free me. I could hear her voice crying out for my safe release. She and her workers had been at the home on several occasions when the police would show up. She had protected me. She knew something was wrong. She had seen firsthand that I was being harassed by local police. She immediately knew that I had been arrested and had come to the station. Her words were not heard, and I would remain in custody.

I was grateful to see them both. I was in bad shape, both physically and psychologically. I saw the look in their eyes. I must have looked like a mess. We went home and grabbed my bag to head to the hospital. Upon returning home, I found the Glock 9 mil missing. I thought it odd that on the police report, this gun was not listed as confiscated. I also found my blue bank envelopes; they were empty, other than some checks and deposit receipts. Additionally, my liquor cabinet, which was filled with top-shelf bottles of liquor, all meant for my housewarming, was emptied. I'm not pointing any fingers. I do not know if it was my daughter removing these items, perhaps in an effort to protect me? To be quite frank, I was more disturbed that they, whoever took my guest's liquor, than the money. I can replace the money and the gun. I'd have to ask everyone once again about the liquor they drank. The only other people to have access were the sub-contractor, my daughter, and the Sheriff's deputy. At that moment, I didn't care; I just wanted to get to the hospital and seek treatment for my swollen legs and my badly injured hands. I was just damn happy to have access to my medications and be out of jail.

My sub-contractor left for another job, and my daughter Hillary was left to take me to the hospital. I had two seizures en route. Hillary left me at the emergency room; she needed to pick up her son. She mistakenly let the Boerne police know this. This was a critical mistake. Once at the hospital, I told the staff I had been without anti-seizure and blood clotting meds for an extended period of time. I also showed them my hands and the damage caused the day before by the police. X-rays were taken, and thankfully, my hands were not broken.

The images showed acute soft tissue damage caused by the handcuffs. I also had the swelling in my legs assessed and felt some relief that I would soon receive the much-needed treatment for my legs and hands. I was mistaken.

Within hours, two police officers dragged me out of the emergency room, and I was placed in the back of a squad car. This one had a solid plastic separator in the back as well as the one separating the front. Just on the other side was an assault rifle painted in gaudy colors. If they thought this was going to frighten me...they had another thing coming. I was dismayed. Hadn't I just checked into the E.R. for treatment? Why were two police officers arresting me? I would later gather the hospital records from that fateful night, in which it was documented that I was not causing any problems within the emergency room. I posed no threat. The damage to my hands was documented, as well as the edema in my legs. Why, then, and who called those police officers? This remains an unanswered piece of this puzzle.

I would later learn that Dr. V. received a call from the investigator on this case, a call she recorded. In this call, he asked about the nature of my seizures. She explained to him in great detail the exact nature of seizures and the difference between mini-mal, semi-mal, and grand mal seizures. How a patient may act during such seizures and that said patient will probably not remember any of the details of the event. He didn't like what she had to say; she eventually became frustrated with his call and informed him that when he had twelve years of medical school and was qualified to practice medicine in two countries, they could talk. That was the end of the conversation. That interview was never entered into evidence; it was never shared with my attorneys, the judge, or the prosecutors, to the best of my knowledge. I would later get six years of probation.

The officers who picked me up at the hospital transported me to S.A.B.H. in San Antonio, Texas. Once there, I was placed in a secure unit. It became apparent to me early on that I was once again "labeled." I would be treated as a sick individual with no rights and given very little dignity. I asked to see a medical doctor to discuss my seizure disorder and was denied this privilege. The very fabric of my soul deceased to exist.

I spent over two weeks on this particular unit. It was frigid cold, my Reynaud's was in full bloom, and the pain in my fingers and toes was excruciating. I had been prescribed Nitro-Bid, a form of nitroglycerin, to increase circulation and thus ease the pain. The facility offered me my Nitro-Bid for three days only; they then discontinued it, and I was left to deal with the pain. I many times joked with my fellow patients, who were also complaining of the cold, that it was as cold as a morgue and that we were all simply dead and didn't know it. This place was so surreal, you could almost believe it. I was told when to sleep, eat, take part in a group, and how to behave. I was no longer a human. I was a statistic. I remained completely compliant for fear of retribution. During our brief outdoor time once or twice a day, I smoked cigarettes with my fellow patients. I borrowed cigarettes until my daughter delivered a pack to the facility. I made my pack a "community donation," only to run out quickly and be right back at begging from others. I had nothing of my own; the suitcase I had packed for the hospital, my two Louis Vuitton bags, and all my belongings had been confiscated.

Four days into my stay, I requested a meeting with the patient advocate. The next day, a patient advocate, Chase, paid me a visit. We met in a private room, and I shared with him some of the atrocities I had witnessed, unspeakable things done to other people, and I also shared the way in which I had been treated. He responded with caring and kindness and gave me access to my wallet, my two bags, my two phones, and my suitcase. I was shocked when I opened my Tumi suitcase. The items I had packed for my hospital stay had gone through, and much was missing. The nightgowns, recently purchased at Niemen Marcus, were gone; my Yves Delorme robe was missing, as were my La Perla bras and panties. I want to say nothing about my skin products, which were prescribed by my doctor.

My Gucci combat boots were missing, and to make matters worse and add insult to injury, my one pack of cigarettes had been emptied and filled with half-smoked cigarettes. There was nothing I could do about the lost items, so I focused my attention on my wallet. I needed to call my new credit card companies and let them know where I was at. To my shock, one of the credit cards had one hundred and sixty thousand plus in charges since my incarceration. I reported this to Chase. I was helpless, and I needed him to step in and truly play the role of patient advocate.

One thing that was not missing was a small bottle of T.H.C. gummies that I had purchased in New Mexico during my cross-country trip with my bodyguard to find my dog. I had not eaten any. This is simply not something I do. I must be honest here. I took the bottle, along with what was left of my personal belongings, back to my room. Now, what to do...What was I to do with these gummies? Here I was in a mental hospital with gummies? I did what came naturally. Being the generous person that I am, I shared. There were a select few women on the unit with me: women who were intelligent, business leaders in our community, and women who, for all purposes, truly should not have been in such a place. I had struck up a friendship with this group during cigarette breaks. We'd discuss local business and politics and work together. I mentioned the gummies, and we were off to the races. Before you knew it, we were all laughing and enjoying one another's company on an entirely new level. The gummies I had were the type that bring a new level of mental acuity, not the type that dumbs you down. We had so much damn fun.

One afternoon, I was witness to an attempted murder of one of the patients on the unit. I heard a commotion and screaming from down the hallway. Initially, I assumed there was a fight, although I heard no code green over the intercom, and if there was a fight, I was all in. I'm not afraid of a good fight; I'm also the one who breaks up many fights in the unit. I have stood between rival factions and been willing to take one for the team. Each and every time I did this, there was never a fight, and thankfully I never got my ass beat.

Early in my stay, for four days to be exact, I was summoned before a judge, a prosecutor, and a civil defense attorney. During our Skype visit, the prosecutor did his best to make me out to be an insane woman. Ranting at me all sorts of accusations, a man that had never met me and who knew nothing of me. The judge overruled him. The judge ordered me released, stating that if I simply played by the rules, I would be home soon. I was given the documents just hours before the meeting. In those documents were the signature and affidavit of the doctor I had never seen. She stated that I had undergone a psychological examination and that it was her opinion I remain in the custody and care of the facility. It would be weeks before I was released and saw the light of day.

I crossed paths with this doctor a day later. When she asked to speak with me privately in my room, I declined stating that all those in attendance, my fellow patients included, were aware of the situation. I looked her straight in the eyes and asked her how she could sign said documents when she had never even seen me, much less performed a psych eval? She had no response; she retreated like a coward. They'll give M.D.s out to anybody these days.

An event, one of many that occurred at S.A.B.H., was especially terrifying. An elderly woman lay sleeping in her bed when her roommate, a much younger woman, attempted to choke her. The screams I heard were those of anguish and utter fear. I flung open the door and viewed the situation. Several of the attending staff were running down the hall; the elderly woman sat motionless on the hall floor, and several other patients were looking in wonder. Later, as the victim of this incident and several of my fellow patients were joined together in the day room, I offered to help the woman who had been assaulted. I had in my possession a copy of all those kept on the unit; it included names and other identifying information. Out of respect, I had never looked at that list and certainly would never view a patient's private information. As I looked down at the list of names, calling each one out in an effort to identify her attacker, I was called out by two of the patients. They took issue with my having the list and thus reported me. I was taken from my room and placed in a men's unit. A very rough place to be. There were three other women there. Things were going south, quick.

I bear witness to another event; this one took place at approximately 3 a.m. in the first unit where I had been placed. Another elderly woman in her seventies, who had been sleeping in the hallway, awoke and was yelling out profanities; she was obviously having a psychotic episode. Her "sitter" watched as an attendant dragged her into a meeting room, a place that was kept even colder than the unit. There she was, placed on the floor, stripped of her clothing, but what was worse, I watched as the attendant entered the room carrying two syringes. I have no idea what was in those syringes; I can only guess what was. The woman was administered both shots. Her shouts began to dim and became moans; then, she fell silent.

Life in the second unit was interesting, to say the least. I immediately identified a gang member. I knew I would be safer in his care than in the care of my fellow patients or the staff. I also thought he was a kind soul. It took a while, but he warmed up to me and soon began sharing his life, his love, and his entire story with me at length. I also made friends with a female member of the Mexican mafia. Again, she was a "safe" choice. I would later be housed in an even more abusive unit, and this friendship would come in very handy.

Then, just two days into my stay, things changed in a heartbeat. I kindly asked one of the staff members if there was someplace I could shower as the shower was broken in my room. My belongings were hastily thrown into a paper sack, and I was briskly escorted to another unit. On the walk over to the unit, staff jokingly stated that I would love the new unit and that the residents talked a lot. I thought things couldn't be any worse than where I had already been. I was wrong; things were about to get very dicey. I was heading to the maximum-security unit, a place where the "real crazies" are held, their basic human rights violated, and their patient rights completely overlooked. I was about to be housed in a unit for the truly insane.

I made a secret vow, with my mind and my heart, that should I ever escape from this place, I would use my voice and my following to end the suffering I witnessed in this hellhole. Don't get me wrong, there are people who need appropriate psychiatric help, and then there are others, the mothers, wives, and sisters that I came to know should not have been so brutally incarcerated. It's false imprisonment, and anyone involved in putting these innocent souls here is subject to a five thousand dollar fine or one year in county jail. That's the law, not Celia Belt speaking.

I know that most of those I met will go home broken, back to their "real" world. Most will be far too intimidated to ever seek relief for their mistreatment. Many enter homeless shelters, or go on to full time care facilities, leaving them with the much-needed medical assistance they require.

Moving on, why I was placed in this high-security unit, for what reason, I will never know. Because the shower was not working in the previous unit? Regardless, I spent nearly five weeks total at S.A.B.H. I was told that a doctor would see me daily when, in fact, no doctor ever came until the day before I was released, other than my brief chat with the doctor in the hall of the first unit. Spending time on this particular unit was quite an experience. I saw and witnessed things that were sometimes amusing and, at other times, deeply disturbing. I laughed on many occasions stating, "You can't make this shit up." The truly disturbed "crazies" on the unit provided continual amusement. I got to the point where I began to state, "I'm staying! Free room and board and great entertainment."

Life wasn't all bad at the hospital. There was the continual entertainment of the crazies, the well-thought-out group sessions, and a few staff members who were kind and truly understanding. One, Michelle, was a true badass. I half dreaded, and half looked forward to her shifts. She made it quite clear that she would not put up with any shit. I admired her strength, her fortitude, and her attitude. After our first rounds together, she began to warm up to me. I was, quite honestly, disappointed that I had been booted off the first unit, assuming I'd not see her again. I caught a brief glimpse of her while in the men's unit. Still, she was not assigned to that detail. Once in the security unit, a few days in, who arrives for her shift...It was Michelle in all her badass glory. She began her work as she always does, telling the patients how things were going to be done and that she would tolerate none of their shenanigans. One day, during a treasured and well-earned cigarette break, Michelle turned to me and said... "You know, Celia Belt, you're all right, I like you." I think of Michelle often. I pray her health has improved, and I hope she was able to open the business she dreamed and spoke of. I would have enjoyed having her on my team and included in my new business. She is an asset and a blessing to all who come to know her.

The thought crossed my mind, as I observed those poor souls around me, isn't insanity perhaps another word for enlightenment? My heart ached for all those who had been imprisoned in such a place, and I wondered how I could possibly be of some service to them. I had to find the silver lining. Why would the Gods allow me such an experience and so much torment? I could only think it was yet another lesson in this lifetime of mine. I must help those who do not have a voice, just as I had helped thousands of burn survivors. This new path, this journey, was mine to embrace. Why, or why, have I been imprisoned? Yes, Ahlab put me here; she has succeeded; however, is there a higher purpose to this pain and suffering of mine? Am I to feel and see all this pain and suffering for a real and very purposeful reason, one for which I do not yet understand?

When I did finally secure my release, the first thing I did was call a man. His wife, Elizabeth, was in the secured unit, and he had no way of knowing where she was or how to contact her. His voice was full of relief and gratitude for my call. It warmed my heart to offer some comfort to this man. I shared with him just how special his wife was and that she was being held in a very bad place.

One thing I made clear to my fellow patients was that if and when I was released, I would help them get word outside of those cold walls. I also shared my name with several of them, stating that they could simply Google "Celia Belt" and follow the next chapter. I was set on changing the world, and I knew that this book would be key to that. If I have just one last breath in me, it will be to pronounce that those held in psychiatric facilities against their will someday be heard. I will also denounce police violence and the false imprisonment of others. I am a widow, living alone. I should not have been manhandled twice in my private residence by police officers. I should not have been falsely imprisoned in mental facilities for what? For having seizure disorder? A diagnosed side effect of a traumatic brain injury. The cries of those I've met are not in vain. I will be their voice, their face, and their champion.

The Gods have plans for me. Am I risking my own life by going so public? Perhaps. I do not fear death. I've coded three times in this lifetime, and I know that Randy is waiting on the other side for me. I will, and I must do the right thing. Going public with my somewhat embarrassing ordeal is the only way I can achieve this. I am not looking for vindication or retaliation. I seek justice for all those who do not possess a voice or a platform. The gods gave me the heart of a Warrior, and I plan on using it.

Just days after returning home, I booked a flight to Seattle. I knew Taboo, my male German Shepherd, was there, and I was planning on facing Trish in court and asking her, under oath, where Risqué was. That plan didn't quite work out. I called the Boerne police and chatted with Sgt. Swift discussing the need to file yet another police report on the missing dogs. They had dropped the original report. Why, I'll never know. This was a grand larceny case, quite serious, and they should have followed up on my case. Regardless, I pulled together my courage, knowing I may be walking into a hornet's nest, and made plans to visit the police station the next day, per her request. I asked my buddy Jimmy if he could go; he flat-out did all he could to dissuade me from going, stating that it was likely a trap.

I also contacted a friend of mine; he was a former judge in a neighboring county. I let him know where I was going, my reason, and the address. He also felt it was a bad idea. That would be the last they heard from me for months. It was a trap; the police had called my daughter Hillary in, and they were questioning her in the next room. She dutifully did so, was questioned, and filled with terror. After some time, the police looked at her and said, "We're going to arrest your mother." I was in the next room, unaware that they had my daughter in for questioning at the same time, assuming I was reopening the report on the theft of my dog. All they seemed focused on discussing was the police brutality report from December of 2022. Report # B2205344.

I requested that Officer Swift be brought in for questioning; she had, after all, been present in the emergency room for several hours following the December incident. If they were so set on discussing this case, perhaps they should be speaking with her. Certainly, she could help clear this up. Officer Swift arrived, sat down, and flatly denied that she had been in the E.R. with me that day. When I reminded her that she had called my daughter, viewed my bruised and bloodied arms and legs, and spoken with staff in the emergency room, her memory appeared to fail her. At this point, I knew I was being set up. They had received a call from my daughter-in-law, Betty, stating that I had a gun in my possession. I simply wanted the case regarding my dogs reopened; I was not there to discuss the December assault. Then, several officers burst through the door and demanded the keys to my car. I had my keys taken from me and my car searched. I was served no search warrant. I thought to ask for onc, but I didn't want to question their authority. I was afraid. In my car, they found a 9mm Rueger Hellcat owned by a friend of mine. He had placed it in my car just days before, unloaded.

I was handcuffed, treated poorly, and carted off to the county jail. I never knew Hillary was in the other room or what she had been put through. She shared this information with me at a later time. The agony she felt was real. She had done nothing wrong; they had placed her in a position to entrap me, and the pain and suffering they caused my daughter would last a lifetime. Betty, my daughter-in-law's actions, left Boerne police with no other alternative but to bring Hillary in and question her. The damage they did to my daughter on that day is unforgivable. I would later learn that Betty, my eldest son Justin's wife, had called the police and told them I had a gun. She had betrayed me and my family and caused us much pain. Why she did this, I can only speculate. I had, just two years before, purchased a home for her and given her family one hundred thousand dollars to pay down their debt. I knew she had her eyes on my estate and was securing her rights to Guardianship over me just as Ahlab did. Sick and twisted, they both were.

To make matters worse, my car was impounded, which was a financial hardship for sure. I was fortunate that my friend Venomara had the foresight to see that we needed to get the car released as soon as possible so we would not incur any more charges. I'm grateful that she did so, as I would end up spending months in jail. Needless to say, I never made it to Washington, to face Trish in a courtroom and confront her as to the whereabouts of Risqué. Once again, they seemed to have won.

The police issued a search warrant for the next day, in my home they found the gun case for the Rueger Hellcat and the receipt for the purchase of the gun, in Tink's name. They confiscated this and the case of the Glock 9 mil that they had taken during my seizure on January 9'th when police arrested me at my home. They did not originally report taking the Glock, it wasn't until later, during my subsequent arrest, when I brought the subject up, that a report was made for the seizure of this gun.

To this day, there is no record, I was never charged with possession of this gun and it's anybody's guess where it is.

Perhaps it's my own ignorance here, but I thought that the unloaded gun in my possession, the Hellcat, with Tink's prints all over it, registered in his name. The police had a copy of this registration. That this gun would not and could not be used against me. I guess I don't know the law. Because, as it ended up, I got six years probation for having that gun in my car. What hurt the most was when I mentioned this to Tink; all he had to say was nothing. He didn't say, "Sorry, I shouldn't have given you that gun," or "I know the laws, I should have known better," or just something, damn it, he should have said something. But he said nothing. I was fined seven thousand dollars plus in court costs and fines and six years probation. I am a convicted felon. And he said nothing.

Months later, through my investigators, it was discovered that Ahlab and her co-conspirators had been calling the Boerne police department the day before my seizure. Stating I was making threats towards them. These were false statements, to be sure. They also made a post on Facebook, claiming it was my post, which it was not. The police were acting off of this false information when they entered my home on January 9th, 2023. If you follow the breadcrumbs, it all leads back to Ahlab, Trish, Tubbs, and Ned. They had now involved law enforcement, and I was about to pay a heavy price.

Betrayal

I was getting back to my new norm. The house was still a wreck. During my time at S.A.B.H., my new flooring had been installed. Not only did they not finish, but it was also installed incorrectly. What a mess. I hired Home Depot to replace all the flooring and gut, remodel the bathroom, and install new windows. Each and every project was done in the worst of fashion, and I was left to clean up the mess. I set about the task of retrieving my dogs. I knew that Trish had Taboo in Washington; still, I had no idea of the whereabouts of Risqué. My investigators were told by the Boerne Police Department that the missing dog's report # B2205244, which I had filed months earlier, had been dropped. I knew that I'd have to swallow my fear of the police and go down to the station to file another report.

It was a Wednesday. I dressed nicely, donning an understated Giorgio Armani dress. I looked at all the businesses. I took my evidence file with me and was assured by Officer Swift that all would go well. I was escorted into a room and began the interview with Officer Rowe. She anxiously kept revisiting the police brutality case when all I wanted to discuss was the dropped case on my missing dogs and a new case issued. I had booked my flight to Seattle, Washington, for that coming Saturday and had every intention of facing Trish in court, in addition to meeting with detectives and the media. My greatest hope was to fly home with Taboo at my side. I was fitting this trip in just before I was due to arrive in Pittsburg to meet with the Sentara Burn Survivors Foundation and pay a visit to the local burn unit. I needed this missing dog case reopened before I left for Seattle. What happened next is beyond belief.

Always so close to Freedom, Yet, So Far!

Just the day before, my friend and former bow instructor, Tink, had given me a Rueger, hellcat, 9 mil. I remember him checking the slide for me, as I was too weak to do so. He handed me the case; in it was the receipt with his name on it. I placed the hellcat in the jockey box of my car. He gave me this gun out of kindness; he knew the fear I lived in daily. I had been so violated by so many. I told him I would not be in need of any bullets. I had a great fear of handling a loaded gun. Yet, there I was, with a gun, nonetheless, in my car.

I asked Officer Swift to join our meeting to discuss what she saw that day in the Boerne emergency room. She saw the bruises and gashes on my arms and legs. Yet, when asked about the event, she remembered nothing. She went so far as to deny that she even visited the E.R. on that day. I was in total shock. My daughter, emergency room staff, and the facility that was called to take me all had knowledge of her being in the E.R. with me for several hours. Things were certainly taking a downturn.

Then, suddenly and abruptly, an officer entered the room and demanded the keys to my car. I didn't know what to say. I had only recently purchased the vehicle, and several people had access to it. Why would they be demanded entrance? Well, as fate would have it, they found the gun my buddy, Tink Nathan, had given me a 9 mil Hellcat to replace the Glock taken by the Sheriff's deputies. After tearing apart my car (and yes, they left it a mess), they entered the room, put me in handcuffs, and stated they had found a weapon in my car. After some time alone in handcuffs and wondering what my fate might be, I was taken, treated like a common criminal, and transported to the Kendall County Jail.

I was charged with possession of that gun; they never ran prints on that gun. The day later, they issued a search warrant for my home and confiscated the case, which had the receipt with Tink's name on it. I would eventually serve six years probation for this. Now, I don't know all the laws. I'm not going to pretend to. However, should they have run the prints? Should they have run the owner's name? Would that have been of some help to me? I don't know. In the end, I was charged and paid a heavy price.

At the jail, I was booked and placed back into the same cold holding cell I had been in a month earlier. I remained there for two days. I was being held on three felony charges; two had bail, and the third was a no-bond. I was going nowhere soon.

The police issued me a search warrant for my home. I kindly shared with them that the house key was on the Louis Vuitton key ring they had taken from me; there would be no need to break into the home, and I had nothing to hide. I also gave them the combination to my safe. My daughter Hillary dropped all she was doing, which included working on her master's degree in developmental education and being a full-time single parent to a three-year-old boy. She made it to the house just as they were finishing up. She was there to make sure nothing was disturbed and confirm they had proceeded with their search. They did a great job. All was in order; unfortunately, they neglected to return my key to the fob, to myself, or to my family. Sometimes, these things just get lost.

The second day I was in custody, an officer came to my cell and handed me a document. In disbelief, I read the words laid out before me. Ahlab was attempting to gain Guardianship of my estate and my person. The document was executed by Ned, the attorney, and was dated the week before I was arrested. Why was it only now being served to me while I was in the custody of the Sheriff's office, and how did she know I was here? Not only did she seek Guardianship of me and my estate, but she had also taken my bill of rights and deleted each and every one. Replacing them with language that would curdle even the blood of a Viking.

To be specific, she was asking the court for the following:

Permanent Guardianship of the estate of Celia Belt

Permanent Guardianship of the person, Celia Belt

The power to take possession of all my medical needs

The power to have me placed permanently in a state psychiatric facility

The power to object to any necessary medical, dental, and healthcare treatment

Authority to have me sterilized or to have an abortion performed

The power to remove me from my home and place me in a psychiatric facility or nursing home

The power to obtain a social security card in my name

The power to receive funds from the government, including my disability and widow's benefits and any social security benefits, including veterans benefits

The power to apply for food stamps in my name

The power to consent to the administration of psychotropic medications

The power to sign a Do Not Resuscitate Order

The power to transport me to an inpatient mental health facility

In addition, she was asking the court for the following:

As stated on her court documents, Ahlab Dibbern requests the court the following limitations of Celia Belt's rights:

Celia Belt shall no longer have the ability to drive a motor vehicle or to obtain a driver's license

Celia Belt shall no longer have the right to vote in a public or private election

Celia Belt shall no longer have the right to make decisions involving her marital status

Celia Belt shall no longer have the right to make decisions or give consent concerning her medical, dental, and healthcare treatment, including tests, examinations,, or evaluations.

Celia Belt shall no longer have the right to make gifts of real or personal property.

Celia Belt shall no longer have the right to execute a Power of Attorney

Celia Belt shall no longer have the right to purchase, use, own, or possess firearms

Celia Belt shall no longer have the right to enter into contracts

Celia Belt shall no longer have the right to make decisions regarding her residence

Celia Belt shall no longer have the right to seek employment, obtain government assistance, or access government benefits or funds

Celia Belt shall no longer have the right to exercise powers and authority over her person, that is to be given to Ahlab Dibbern

Now, if the above doesn't have you thinking... If a family member could commit such an atrocity on a fellow family member, what can a stranger or an acquaintance do to you?

I should add here that I have always been kind and extremely generous to my cousin Ahlab and her children. Not once have I been cruel or uncaring.

She could have stayed home and raised the children on my dime. Yet, she got greedy. Needless to say, Ahlab will never receive another dime from me, my children, or my estate. I wish her no harm, nor do I wish her any good.

With his new development, I prepared to face Ahlab and her attorney, Ned in court. I was given an hour to prepare. The dates on the document had been changed to adjust to court schedules. (I'm assuming.)

I met with my court-appointed attorney via Skype just hours before the court hearing. It was our first meeting. It didn't take her long to figure out that something was really wrong and perhaps crooked with this entire case. She suspected the attorney, Ned, of something. I met her at the courthouse. We entered the room, and Ned, my old attorney, now Ahlab's, sat there, looking quite smug. He had brought with him the notary who had signed the falsified P.O.A. that Ahlab had been using to seize my assets.

I was dressed in a black and white striped prison uniform. I arrived at the courthouse with shackles on my legs and a chain around my waist that held the tight handcuffs in a secure fashion. My attorney popped in for a brief meeting; it was her suggestion that we allow the orders to go through and appoint Ahlab as my "temporary" guardian until the next court appearance, at which time permanent Guardianship would be awarded. I flatly refused. I would take my chances with the judge, hoping and praying he had read all the documents and could see the exact nature of what Ahlab and her attorney were attempting to achieve. The shackles and chain were removed before I entered the courtroom. There I stood, in handcuffs with my prison garb, yet I didn't feel powerless. I was powerful. By the grace of the Gods, the temporary order was not approved; however, we still had the threat of the permanent order going to court. I was ordered to undergo a psychiatric and competency evaluation by a doctor chosen by Ahlab's attorney, (Ned) and the date was set for the next hearing. It was all up to me to prove my sanity, stand up to Ahlab and her crew, and keep myself sane in the meantime. I'm a warrior, through and through.

The night before the competency evaluation, I was called by the guards to meet with my attorney; I found this odd, as I had already spoken with her. I was escorted out to the small rooms that are reserved for attorney meetings. As I sat and waited, I was shocked when Ned arrived, Ahlabs' attorney. Now, this is highly unethical. Regardless, I played along. He had five thousand dollars that I had previously paid him to represent me. I addressed that issue first. He agreed to return the money to me, and then we began to address the guardianship issue. It was apparent that he was there to intimidate me. I was not about to allow that to happen. I asked him, point blank, if he planned on continuing in this effort to represent my cousin in an effort to pursue Guardianship of my person and my assets. His answer was swift and decisive; yes, he was. With that, the conversation ended; I would see him in court in two days' time after I had undergone my competency evaluation. There is no doubt in my mind that he was there to intimidate me the night before my evaluation in an effort to win his case. My only thought was, *You piece of shit!*

The date for the psych eval was set Wednesday. I busied myself reading and getting to know my new bunkmates in "pod B."" There were eight of us. All but me was a meth or heroin user, and all but me had seen time in the penitentiary. Among them were two ring leaders; both were bullies. I observed them manipulate their fellow inmates. I remained detached and uninvolved until it became personal. For no earthly reason, one of these bullies got in my face, calling me old and threatening me with bodily harm. I remained calm and waited for her tirade to end, and then I calmly stood, looking her in her eyes, telling her she was out of line. She backed down at that point; however, her abusive attitude toward me never ended. The second bully was also verbally abusive and attempted to stir up trouble within the pod, claiming I was responsible for many things, which I was not. She took it a step further and dumped out an entire bottle of shampoo I had only recently purchased through the commissary. I remained calm until her verbal attacks on my person were well out of line. I responded with one statement... "Stand down."

The day of my exam was fast approaching. I stood firm in the knowledge that I was a sane, self-sufficient human being and that I would pass the medical exam. I did, however, have some doubts: Was the doctor, referred by Ahlab's attorney, the same attorney, mind you, that I had hired and paid, a fair and ethical doctor? Was my court-appointed attorney on my side? Did she truly care, or was I just another in the long line of defendants she had represented?

Enter Lacey Barriga, my court-appointed attorney. I owe her the world. She saw through the diabolical scheme that Ahlab and her attorney were up to. She protected me. Regardless, I still needed to do well on the exam to foil their plot. Dr. Jason Schillerstrom, MD, was set to administer the exam. Lacey and I met with the doctor, one of his interns, and a med student who was along for the ride. As the test began, I felt a total calm transcend my body and mind. I was Celia Belt. I could and would care for myself. Ahlab's intention was to deem me incompetent. That would not be the case. I not only passed the test. I completed it with a very high level of intelligence and with pure grit. A day later, as I was speaking with my daughter, she informed me that I had passed the exam. The court case against me would be dropped. I had dodged one bullet; I had several more hurdles to cross. I hoped and prayed this would be the last I heard of Ahlab. I never wanted to hear her name again.

As I adjusted to life in Pod B, I found amusement in the smallest of things. I also sought solace, for I was locked up in a small area with seven other convicts, locked up away from all the comforts of home, isolated from friends and family. The thought occurred to me that beyond our locked door, there was another locked door, and outside of that were two more locked doors that one must enter through to achieve freedom. I had to put the thought away, or I would certainly lose my mind.

The cold is tough to describe. It's bone chilling, a freezing cold. Is this what it feels like to be in a coffin? I lived in four layers of clothes, and slept with two blankets. I was allowed an extra blanket due to my Reynauds disease. Even with these extra layers, I was constantly shivering. I made a vain attempt to get the shower as hot as possible and stand there begging for some relief. I'd then wrap myself tightly in my layers of clothes, then in the blankets, tucking them tightly around my body and head, hoping for some relief from the biting cold. We were constantly asking the guards to turn the air down, to please turn the heat on, for some unknown reason, this never came to pass and we would suffer in silence.

Amusement came in the way of my fellow inmates, their stories, and life events. Many of these women had substance abuse issues, some had children and families back home. Several were dangerous; this was obvious to me and I would need to act with caution. They all had stories to tell. The room also contained a television. I had not watched T.V. for many years, and the funny movies we occasionally watched offered a bit of a reprieve from my current situation. As the low duck in the pecking order, I was not allowed to choose a station. I was grateful for any bit of diversion and especially happy when someone would choose something amusing to watch.

My fellow inmates had quite a different schedule than I was accustomed to. I'm a morning person. My fellow inmates slept quite long hours, and I was not allowed to watch the T.V. with any sound during morning hours; this, many times, stretched into lunchtime and even into dinner due to their sleep. I spent my time reading and coloring. Doing all I could to remain quiet.

After some time, I was able to maneuver the remote and found the closed caption button, thus allowing me to read the text. Of course, this was not fully my option as I had not yet received the glasses my daughter had dropped by. I spent most of my days standing close to the T.V. and reading what I could. I also spent a great deal of time coloring. My daughter ordered me an intricate coloring book from Amazon, as we were not allowed to read our own books. The first, *Empowering Goddesses*, provided hours of delight and intense work. The second, *Fragile World*, took me to the world of endangered species. Many I had hunted in Africa or had come across my ranch in Bandera or my home in Boerne. I was entranced. The intricate detail and outlines of the pictures offered me an escape from the dim world I found myself in, a reprieve of sorts. I ordered some colored pencils from the commissary and filled the pages with vivid colors. There were only twelve colors in the pack, so I had to expand my mind, mixing colors, outlining, and shading to create a palette of color.

The second book she sent, *Fragile World*, offered an even more challenging spectrum of designs. I spent hours creating my masterpieces, sharing them with fellow inmates, and simply looking at what I had created. Hillary was eventually able to get a word search sent to me, once again, via Amazon. I waited days for the guards to process the book, and once it was in my hands, I set about the task of completing each puzzle. Allowing my mind to be tested, each word opening up a new memory. I was not surprised that my daughter ordered books that were of a high level for me, meaning they were difficult! She also sent me books authored by Max Lucado. I knew Max and his wife, Denalyn. Our children attended the same prep school, and I attended a prayer group with Denalyn. I couldn't help but think, I wonder what Max would think of me, kicking back on my metal cot, taking in his words of wisdom, in a jail cell. I was grateful for those words; they helped keep me alive.

My sixty-first birthday was fast approaching. I was sure I'd be released in time to spend it with family and friends. I could not wrap my head around the thought that I would actually spend another holiday away from my family. Yet, as the day grew closer, I had to accept the fact . My cellmates, however, made it so special for me. Julia colored a picture for me using stickers from a deodorant bar to wrap it, Angel made a dip out of the rice and beans I'd purchased through the commissary, and best of all, they all sang happy birthday to me. It was one of my best birthdays ever. I will never forget those girls and thc laughter we shared. That night as I lay in bed, tears streamed down my face as I thought of my daughter, my son and my grandson.

The day came when Hillary mentioned on the phone that she had found an attorney; she had vetted him well and felt he would be a good fit for my case and that he would work with us regarding our current financial situation. That attorney's name was Steven Berrarra, and he has been my angel from that day forward. I have had several angels enter my world during this experience; another came in the form of my bond company, Megan and Lacey, a mother-and-daughter team- they ran Alright Bond company. They were familiar with who I was and had admired my horses out at my ranch in Bandera. Again, nothing is by coincidence. In our first conversations, they were aghast as to why I was being held with “no bond”, they saw no good reason for this. They took a personal interest in me and my case and helped put my mind at ease during some truly rough days. When the time came, and I finally was granted a bond, it took every dime I had in the bank and selling a few valuables to make it all work, but we did it! I was set free on a Friday afternoon. Little did I know that I would return to my cell just two days later.

Bestir

On March 13th, I woke to a glorious day, home and free at home. My daughter arrived to collect me and take me to my "check-in" at pretrial services. Little did I know, they were waiting for me. My ankle monitor had not been charged. I was unaware that it required a daily charge, I thought it needed a charge every Wednesday, I was wrong. They knew I had no access to phones because the police had taken all three of my phones, and the internet was mysteriously not working at home. Now, they did have my daughter's phone number, yet they did not call her to inquire as to why the ankle monitor had gone dead.

They waited until I showed up dutifully to pretrial, all dolled up for my first appointment. I waited for three long hours as they had me charge my ankle monitor. The staff waited with me, informing my daughter to leave me there, that they were unsure of my fate, and the decision was in the D.A.'s hands. Hillary came in at this point, taking my purse, my bank envelope containing checks in need of deposit, and any other valuables I had on my person. I knew at that moment that she knew, although she had not been told of my fate, she knew in her heart that her mother was in real danger. She feared that I was soon to be arrested and that I would once again be a resident of the county jail. The pain I saw in her eyes was penetrating.

It was a tortuous three hours, yet what could I do but stand there, alone, charging my ankle monitor. Hillary never returned for me. At one point, I asked the pretrial officer to please ring my daughter, but I was worried about her making the long trip to my bank in Bandera. I was told by the officer that my daughter was simply running late when, in actuality, she had been informed of my soon-to-take-place arrest. She was driving home with my grandson, tears running down her face. Time dragged by as I stood with my monitor charging. I called my attorney, and explained the situation to him, he immediately contacted the D.A.'s office and went to work. Hours passed, and as I looked out at the highway, I noticed a local squad unit taking the exit leading to our location. I waited, and within minutes, the same car appeared in the parking lot. I greeted them in a friendly fashion as they entered the pretrial office. I was still praying that their reason for being there was something else. Certainly, I would not be arrested for simply not charging my ankle bracelet.

As they tapped on the door, my pretrial officer appeared; she looked at the officers and, pointing to me, said, "This is Celia Belt." I was handcuffed behind my back and placed in the hard back seat of a squad car. Once again, I was on my own, alone. The fear was real, and the tears were streaming down my face in torrents. The entire time, the pretrial staff were on the phones with my attorney and the D.A.'s office, and my daughter was in and out. They all knew the terrible truth. I was going back to that living hell they call jail. I was able to make one call out to my attorney. I wept as I spoke to him, pleading... "I did nothing wrong." His calm voice gave me some comfort, yet in the end, his efforts to save me were fruitless. I was arrested and placed back in jail, where I would spend the next two months. Most of my time was spent in solitary confinement in the Kendall County Jail.

My attorney assured me this was a simple mistake and that I should be released on bond soon. Kendall County has but one judge, a good one at that, and as luck would have it, she was in the midst of a jury trial. This was going to mean that my time in jail would be extended. I swallowed a hard pill that day. Those words were hard to hear. I had become a victim of the system, and I would have to wait and sit. I was initially placed back into pod B with my former cellmates. I jokingly said, "I'm back," as I reentered the room and took a hard steel bunk. In only a matter of days, things got a bit rough in the pod; two of my fellow inmates, one of whom was detoxing off meth, and the other, a single mother who had been in jail for seventeen months. I had been in the pod with the latter of the two previously and had an incident with her, at which time I stood my ground and earned her respect. This time, things were different. She had an ally that was more than willing to demean me every chance they got. It was brutal and constant torment from the moment they woke until they slept. They included the guards in this.

I was eventually removed from the pod and placed in solitary. All involved thought I was being punished when truly, I was damn happy to be out of there. I was asked to pack up, which I did. I sat by the door for hours as I was ridiculed and bullied by my cellmates. I remained calm with the knowledge that I was soon to be moved. I dragged my plastic mattress and my few belongings down the hall and was shown into a small room with no windows. The large steel door was closed soundly behind me. I looked around me, the room, a seven by ten enclosure, with no windows, a toilet and shower, all was filthy with a metal bunk that was covered in food crumbs, this was my new home. I had best start cleaning. I was not allowed to attend church, go to rec, or go to the library. The simplest of pleasures I had enjoyed were no longer mine. Simple pleasures, yet they were pleasures to me.

I stayed in that room for three weeks with no human contact. Weeks became months. I was eventually allowed to go to rec and the occasional church meeting, albeit most times alone. The closest thing I had to human interaction was a slot in the door that opened three times a day. A tray was passed through with food if that's what you'd call it. No sound, no laughter, no talking, just the chirp of the crickets that made their way up through the drains each night. I had to remember the titles of my first two books...*Remarkably Intact* and *Silent Warrior*. For in those days, I certainly was both.

As I looked about the cement walls and the steel appliances, a memory came to me, the deriding tanks of my youth. I was derided after being burned as an infant in tanks, a memory that was long tucked away, a memory that should never be remembered. Yet, here it was, this place was bringing it back. The close quarters of this place, the door slamming, everything about this place brought back that terrifying memory. I knew I had to fight to keep it away. I had to survive this; somehow, I knew I had to live, or I'd die. I shared this with Nurse Mac, and the only solution she had was to offer me medication that might help with the stress of P.T.S.D. I didn't want to take it. However, I saw no other solution when she told me it would probably be months before I was released from that cell. The thought of months in that isolation cell, with those memories, was more than I could bear, so I agreed, and I took the medication.

The guards are trained to make your life a living hell. Jail is not supposed to be fun, folks; it's there as a punishment. They do their job, and they do it damn well. They made several attempts to intimidate me, treat me like shit, and do some pretty nasty things to me. All is forgiven in my mind; they are simply there to do a job. I respect that. I expected no special attention. I was assured it would be rough, and it was. I'm sure many of them thought I would break down once I'd been placed in solitary confinement, the "hole," as it's called. I'm not sure how people do exist in those conditions. All I do know is that somehow, I did survive. I lost forty-one pounds, most of my hair, and shed a fair number of tears. I busied myself doing pushups against the wall, whistling, and constantly cleaning my room. I was averaging seven thousand pages a week reading, and lord knows how much coloring I did. I was consumed with the written word and with creating color out of my twelve pencils. I did all I could to amuse myself and to remain sane. I had to survive this.

In my mind, I Wore a Dress of Anguish.

My daughter and friends sent me a good supply of books and challenging coloring books. One of the books was in French, and I began learning the language in jail. My mind drifted to stories my daughter had shared with me of her visit to France, the people and the topography. The big excitement each week was Wednesday; that was commissary delivery day. Anthony, a kind and thoughtful guard, would unload my array of purchases and I would take great care in organizing each item. It was a way to pass the time. It also brought great comfort to know I would have food and toiletries for the upcoming week. Simple things became so important. The second most exciting days were Monday and Friday, the days we were allowed access to our razors. You learn to treasure the little things in life.

My buddy, Tink Nathan, Venomara, my son Jarred, and my daughter all made sure I had plenty of money in my account to purchase all I needed. Not that the commissary offered any fruit or vegetables. I could feel my body lacking the basic nutrients, I studied the nutritional facts of labels, looking for any way to sustain myself. I discovered that Lays potato chips offer fifteen percent of vitamin C per day. That would be my one way to obtain some way of securing some vitamin C and I began eating them daily. I was blessed to have the ability to purchase some chips, bottled water, and shampoo. There's not much you can do in jail to maintain a proper diet, I had to become creative.

With so little available to me, I became inventive. I purchased some hair tonic for black people, which is high in vitamin E and mixed with an anti-inflammatory cream. I was given each day some water, a good dose of body lotion, and Folgers coffee, which I'd purchased through the commissary. I used this to reduce the swelling in my feet, my ankles and legs. I was not allowed to see surgical treatment for this pulmonary condition. The swelling had increased dramatically, and it was becoming difficult to walk, not that I had much room to walk around in. Regardless, I needed to reduce the swelling, and my little invention worked! I also purchased a bag of Jolly Ranchers candy; I held these under the shower head to scent the room. I'm here to tell you that it worked; my small cell had the fragrant aroma of green apples.

I've never required much sleep. With the room going black at 10:30, I'd lay awake and listen to the guards laughing and conversing in the adjoining area. Although I couldn't make out what they were saying, I took some comfort in their laughter. Just hearing another human being laugh was like water to this thirsty soul of mine. I was also in close proximity to the detox tanks and heard my fair share of inmates going through the pains of detoxing off of drugs and alcohol. The hours spent vomiting, screaming out in pain, and banging anything they could get their hands on—My Heavens!!! Something I'm thankful I've never had to deal with; it sounds downright gruesome. One night in particular, a woman screamed the entire night, a painful type of scream, seemingly anguished to the point of despair. I couldn't help but wonder who that woman was, if she was missed by loved ones at home, and what she did to come to such a place. I've never lacked empathy. It is something that comes very naturally to me.

I made the most of my brief visits to rec, an area the size of a small basketball court. I did all I could to maintain my muscle mass, doing push ups against the walls, executing my crunches on the hard floors and stretching on the concrete floors, extending my toes and my arms as far as they could reach, and taking brisk walks. I'd whistle as I walked, the songs of birds I had heard from the four corners of the world. Sweet melodies to steer my restless soul, I'd also include the melodies of songs to stir my mind. The guards would many times leave me for extended periods of time, this I was most grateful for, I would then position myself on the floor, meditate for long periods of time, then stretch out, peeling it out, as if by layers. Looking through the caged ceiling, I would occasionally catch sight of a bird. I could not help but wonder, does the wind beneath his wings take him to my home, just a few short miles away? Does he see me there, caged like an animal, unable to fly?

I knew I had to endure whatever suffering was about to come. I had to survive, not only for myself but for those I love and those I serve. There were many nights I felt I was taking my last breath. I had to remind myself that the last breath of this life is the first breath of the next life. That is what kept me alive. That breath.

As my time was extended and I became more of a permanent fixture at the jail, my sick sense of humor began to show through. I just couldn't help myself. My old adage... Laugh, you live...Cry, you die. I was begging to be heard, and sure as shit, I began to have some fun. A few of my escapades included jacking with the guards and Nurse Mac. God love her; she was so much fun to mess with. Twice a week, we were given clean uniforms. I called them my "costumes". Well, I wrote the word SLAVE on the front of mine, in italic bold print, for all to see. I wore that costume to church, to use the kiosk, and for my rec time. Referring to my cell as the white trash bed and breakfast was also an ice breaker and the guards found it quite amusing. In addition I had some great fun with Nurse Mac each morning. It was all done in good humor; nothing was meant to offend, only to put a smile on people's faces and lighten the mood. I'm not sure if my antics were always viewed that way by the guards on duty or those listening in to every phone call I made from my cell.

There were many nights, as I lay in that dark cell, that I thought I was drawing my last breath. I had lost a significant amount of weight, and without proper medical care, I was declining. My friends Venomara, Tink, and Jimmy were of constant support, as was my daughter. I knew I was on the edge. I allowed myself that one last breath and then breathed another. I reminded myself that the last breath of this life is the first breath of the next. It mattered not, that I may cross over in this seven by ten cell, alone, I would be going home, to Randy. I uttered those words many a night, praying that the Gods heard me and would allow me entry to that next world. I was ready to go, to be in the company of my mother, my baby sister, and my beloved Randy. I was ready.

My dear friend Venomara contacted me and offered a tremendous amount of support not only to myself but also to my daughter. My daughter dealt with a great deal of guilt regarding my being put into jail the second time due to what the police did to her, and Venomara was a true blessing to both of us. Hillary once again began sending me books to read, challenging coloring books to occupy my time, and spending countless hours working on my behalf. She became such a strong advocate, contacting Texas Disability Rights attorneys, numerous advocates and the Texas Jailhouse Project. At one point, Texas Disabilities asked her to speak at a state convention. When the day finally came, and I had my hearing before the judge, I believed with all my heart that a bond would finally be set, and I would be allowed to return home. My attorney, Stephen, sent his associate, Robert Arrelano, to represent me, and I was heart wrenched when the judge said, "No bond." What? No bond? I could not believe what

I was hearing. The judge ordered that I undergo a competency evaluation and a psychological evaluation before she would be granted bail and that she would have this done within the week.

Well, that didn't happen. It would be weeks before the tests were completed, and I was granted another hearing date. Days and weeks were to pass and each day I was not called for the exams. I finally was given the opportunity to be administered the test and I passed both exams. I am competent to stand trial and answer for myself, and I have no serious psych issues. I have a brain injury; I have a seizure disorder, plain and simple. A diagnosed condition dating back to 2017, how difficult is that to diagnose? Why can't our world and the judicial wrap their arms around that? Why is it that they want to immediately categorize someone with seizure disorder as having a mental disorder?

I had asked Hillary to send me a copy of *Remarkably Intact* and *Silent Warrior*. That would be the only way I would have access to my photos. I needed to see those photos. I so badly missed my daughter, my grandson, my son Jarred, and his wife, and I missed Randy. As I was flipping through the pages, reliving history, it occurred to me that other than the editing process, I had never read my own books. Both are short reads. I could certainly fit them in between my books on Eleanor of Aquitaine and a book of poetry Hillary had sent for me. What happened when I read those words was cathartic. My history was laid out before me. The love I had for my family and friends and the dedication to the Moonlight Fund were all lovingly shared between those covers. I also took pleasure at the site of Randy and I together. Whether it was hunting in Africa, kayaking the Red River in Arizona, or dining out in Mexico City. There was true love exuding from those photos, the love of a lifetime. I pondered his face, looking for some signs of my future. Vivid memories flooded my mind, and for a moment, I wasn't in jail, I was free. Was he still with me, and would I ever love him again? I think that will make for a good book someday.

Family and friends helped with the fees for using the phone, and as much as I wanted to hear everyone's voice just a little longer, I had to conserve. We knew that each and every phone call was taped; we had nothing to hide, yet it made for awkward conversations. The phone was attached to the wall at a nice height for the average four-foot-four person; I'm five feet seven inches tall, so I found myself bent over much of the time. A backbreaker on any given day, but those calls meant the world to me. I have a vivid memory of my two Bibles sitting on the small steel table just below the phone. Tears would drip on my Bibles, creating a puddle by the end of more than one conversation. During one conversation, my daughter asked what I was afraid of, in general, just what I was afraid of? My answer was swift and honest. I fear nothing...Nothing...

How I wished those tears could become a stream. I could have cried a stream, a lovely Texas river that I could float down endlessly, just as I had out at the ranch. A river with a loose rock bottom and surrounded by the shade of century-old cypress trees. That's the water I needed. Clean and pure, the type of water that does not corrupt shows no favor, stands in no judgment, water to carry me home.

Many a night, I revisited my time in Africa, that magical land filled with stars at night and the beasts of the day. Randy and I, in the heat of the day and the magic of the night. Making love to him under the stars of the African sky is like no other experience. Our bodies, lying with the sweet sweat of the hunt and the better sweat of our love. I loved that land as I loved him.

We faced much scorn for having been hunters; on many occasions, I had to remind people that we donated four thousand pounds of our kill to a local village, to indigenous Africans who were literally starving. Randy was always finding ways to give in every way of his life. He was a giver, whether it was through my charity work or our hunting. We kept two freezers in our Bandera garage. Visitors never left empty-handed. Axis, elk, dove, whitetail, and hog meat are plentiful in Texas, and we shared our kills with all. We killed for ourselves and others. We rarely used a processor. We field-dressed, skinned, and processed most of our own meat.

On one occasion, close to the Mexico border, we had been dropped off in search of elk. Randy shot a nice buck; we field dressed the carcass and readied it to be dragged up the hill. As dusk turned to blackness, we heard no sound of the ranger. Our friends had busied themselves at the fire pit, and we were left behind, miles from help. We did what came natural to us, we made love in the woods, a long and languid sort of lovemaking, in the black of night, among the wild animals and a cascade of stars that surrounded us. It would be hours before we heard the steady rumble of the ranger approach and viewed the headlights. We were lucky not to run into any illegals crossing the border. This was a dangerous country. Randy and I were both carrying 308s in addition to 9mms. We also had our skinning knives on board. Needless to say...We weren't that worried.

Back in jail, my phone calls were recorded. I had no privacy, even when speaking with my attorneys. All would and could be used against me, a fact I was soon to realize.

During my time in jail, I was incarcerated with a woman, held in a separate area. This said the woman had killed the brother of someone that was dear to me. As I sat with her at a church group, I had to remind myself: You're in jail... I offered her a shoulder to cry on and an ear to listen. I never revealed to her that I knew of the life she had taken. That young lady, just twenty-two years of age, stood trial and was sentenced to twenty years in prison. She was the daughter of a well-known businessman, and her trial was made public. I hope she is well and adjusting to her new norm. I hold nothing against her. The life she took that all rests in the God's hands.

I finally got my day in court on May 11th, 2023. I was granted bail that day. As I looked back, I viewed Venomara, her friend, Tammy, and my beloved daughter... All were in tears. Friends and family pulled together to raise the money and win my freedom, and my buddy Tink Nathan offered to not only pay the bond but also cover the first month's cost of my ankle bracelet. I hated to accept charity from friends. Tink and I go back twenty-six years. He was my bow instructor. A mighty good one at that. He's famous as the inventor of Tink's hunting products, but he's even more famous for his big game kills from around the world. All taken with a bow. He's also the son of one of one of this nation's World War II/Korean War commanders, to say nothing of the fact, he's also a Colonel, a member of the Texas Rangers.

It would be six long days before I saw the sun and took my first breath of fresh air. On May 16th, I walked out of the Kendall County Jail with an ankle monitor on and into the arms of my bondsman, Megan, and my daughter, Hillary. Hugging never felt so good. As odd as this may sound, I felt a bit melancholy, leaving the guards, Nurse Mac, and the staff behind. They had become fixtures in my life. I took my time dressing in the same clothes I'd worn that fateful day over two months before when I was rearrested. I put my rings and watch on, gathered my piles of books, and bid farewell to those guards on duty. One made a comment to me, a goodbye of sorts; I looked at him and said the only thing that came to mind was, "It's been a good ride."

Coming home was a surreal experience. Not only was the house still a construction zone, my daughter and her friends had trashed the place. Not purposely, but just their lifestyle. I was faced with not only having to get the work completed in the house but also cleaning up the mess, both in the yard and the house. To say nothing of the fact that my finances were a mess. I'd had to access what little funds I had left, and with so much going out for bond money and contractors, I was in a world of hurt. I had the added stress of knowing that my attorneys had not yet been paid; they had taken my case pro bono with the understanding and my promise that they would be paid in the future. *Shit, I had some work to do.*

Freedom never felt so good. I awoke on my first morning back home with the sweet Texas sunshine streaming through the windows, warming my face. I gazed out at the pool, hearing the lovely burbling of water features on the tanning ledge. The birds were issuing their first low chirps of the morning, and somewhere off in the distance, I could hear a woodpecker making his way with a stout piece of wood. A dove cooed his sweet song, the sound of love, and I took in the cascading sound of the waterfall into the pool. It felt good to be lying on Yves Delorme sheets, with my down pillows piled high below my head and the comfort of my down duvet nestled up to my shoulders. I had curled up the night before in my new Zero Gravity bed, hit the massage button, and felt like a kitten in its mother's arms. My recently installed seventy-two-inch fan added just the right amount of breeze to the room. I put on my playlist, some Melody

Godot, singing in French, which was just the right touch as I snuggled up with Bobo the Cat, looked out the window, and for the first time in months, I viewed the trees and how they moved in the wind, my first glimpse through a real window. It had been months since I looked out a real window. Glass, I was looking through glass, it was surreal. It was more than I could ask for. I thanked the Gods for blessing me with the simple things. I could once again breathe the fresh air, sit in the sun, and view the stunning moon at night.

It felt so good to pour drops of lavender into the tub and take a nice long bath. I grabbed a fresh jar of shea sugar scrub and prepared for my time spent in splendor. Wait, one problem with this picture. As I prepared to enter my new Jacuzzi tub, which must be at least three feet deep, I realized I still had the monitor on my ankle. There would be no good soak for me. This well-thought-out event would have to wait. I was on house arrest, and the ankle monitor did not allow submersion. I'm not one to spoil myself with such luxuries, yet, here I was, ready for just such a luxury. Amusing what a few months in jail will make you appreciate.

I did live in constant fear. The police had kept a key to the house, and with my previous experience of checking into pretrials, I was certainly on edge. Although my restrictions included not drinking and no internet usage, a curfew, monitored trips, and the ever so tight monitor on my ankle. I could live without much of what I was accustomed to. I had plenty to do with getting my home in order and began the long task of recouping some of my losses. I was picking up the pieces of a broken life, one piece at a time.

I was living with no phones other than a landline that was not working. The police had confiscated all three of my cell phones. Hillary made the twice-weekly trip to the food pantry to supply me with some sustenance. I had no way of seeing emails or any correspondence; my Google was frozen. I later found that Ahlab had gained access to this account. Little by little, I regained some semblance of life. I set up a new email, LinkedIn, Google, and Windows account. That was reassuring, yet I still had no access to my burn survivors across the globe. My heart broke thinking of them, without a means to offer my financial and emotional support. I had been taken down to nothing. Between Ahlab and my incidents with the police, I was lowered to a new standard. But I am a survivor, and I will survive this. I simply had to.

I spent hours cleaning, organizing, and planting flowers. Sitting by the firepit at night, watching a roaring fire and gazing at the amazing moon and stars overhead. I could not help but wonder, are they looking back at me, do the stars know, the journey of my past months, the road I have walked? My mind always goes to Randy when I see the moon, as if he's always just right there, watching over me. He is my moon, and I am his sun. I'm sure he was right there with me, in that cramped, cold cell, holding me tight and whispering in my ear...I love you. How else could I have survived the past eight months?

I'm still alive, I survived, and I may have even thrived during those dark days. What could have broken me, has empowered me.

I was living in a gilded cage. I was not allowed to leave my home, drive my car, visit friends, or dine out. My three cell phones had been taken by the police, and I was not allowed access to the internet. My credit had been destroyed, my social media access denied, and I was, at times, totally bereft. I did, however, have this book to write. I'd be missing my grandson's fourth birthday party. I knew I had a trial approaching for gun possession, and I'd need to be prepared for that. I needed to be the best, healthiest version of myself, both for my friends and my family. I was buoyed by visits from friends, and Hillary came by faithfully, sometimes more than once a day. I'm blessed, and I know it.

My life was moving forward; I was compliant with all the judge had ordered, I lived with a bit of stress in regards to the ankle monitor, and then, one day, it simply did not work. I immediately rang the monitoring company and troubleshooted the device. They informed me that the charger was not functioning and I'd need to purchase a new one. I immediately did so and had it overnighted. I rang the pretrial officer and made them aware of this. It was late in the day, and they demanded that I drive to San Antonio and acquire a new charger. I shared with Officer Moreno that first off, I did not drive, I had no one to drive me, it was late in the day, even if I found a ride, I would probably not arrive before the office closed, and I'd also purchased a new charger that had a guaranteed next morning arrival. She would hear nothing of it. She demanded that I immediately report to the San Antonio location and purchase a new charger. All parties involved thought this demand was simply out of bounds, considering the time and the fact I had already ordered a unit.

The next day, my charger arrived, and I immediately plugged my unit in. I called the ankle monitoring home office and pretrial, and everything seemed in order. We had a court date set for the following week. It was a hearing in which my attorney was to ask that my ankle monitor be removed; rather than this request being heard, the pretrial turned it into a three-ring circus, accusing me of tampering with the ankle bracelet and asking the judge to place me back into custody. They wanted me placed back in jail. I simply could not believe what I was hearing. I was prepared; I had brought the non-functioning charger with me, and the cord was visibly broken. I also brought my receipts and all the email correspondence. My attorney presented this to the judge. Pretrial continued with their verbal attacks on me, dead set on placing me back in jail. The judge listened to both sides, patiently weighing all the facts. She visibly viewed the broken charger.

Then came the time that the prosecutor was given her opportunity to question me; I remember turning in her direction, readying myself to answer her questions, and then it happened. My body began to contort, my legs buckling under me, my eyes diving; I was having a grand-mal seizure right there, in front of the judge, my attorney, the police officers, everyone. I couldn't control my body. I remember very little. I do know that a police officer ran to grab a chair and place it under my body as I was falling. A kind act, for sure. The only real memory I have is of seeing one of the Pretrial staff members covering her eyes. It seemed to last forever. I was attempting to stop it, stop the shaking, control my legs and my arms, and focus my eyes, but I could not. At some point, the judge asked if 911 should be called. I do recall putting my hand up and uttering, NO. When I did finally gain control of my body, my attorney kindly lifted me up, escorted me out of the courtroom. In the hallway, I was joined by my bodyguard, my dog, and my daughter. I used my inhaler in an attempt to get my breath under control. We sat for quite some time. I was both embarrassed and quite shaken up. Then, the terrible thought crossed my mind, did I pee my pants? Thankfully, I had not. I looked down at my Armani dress, already wrinkled due to the episode I had so carefully chosen for this court appearance, my eyes took in my kitten heels, had they been broken during the episode? My attorney explained that we would have to go back before the judge and finish the hearing; I would need to pull myself together. A terrifying thought, indeed.

As I sat in the hallway, one of the prosecutors brought the damaged charger out to me, showing it to me; he insinuated that I had damaged it; I simply looked at him and said, "Why would I do such a thing, and cause myself so much grief and so much harm?" The time arrived, and I was needed back in the courtroom; I was comforted to see my friend, Tink, sitting in the front row; wearing his Texas Rangers shirt, he had seen everything. I was both embarrassed and yet relieved that he was there. As I sat waiting, a police officer approached me; what he said took me back, and I will never forget his words, "Don't do that again; don't have another seizure." Now, if I could control my seizures, don't you think I would? It was so insulting and degrading to hear those words. I simply looked up into his eyes and said, yes, sir.

When my time came to approach the bench, I stood next to my attorney. He once again laid out the facts of the case, including the broken charger incident. The judge listened intently. Once again, it was time for the prosecution to question me, and as I turned their way, I prepared myself emotionally for what was about to come, praying I would not, once again, experience a seizure and that I would answer all and any questions they might have for me. As I looked into the eyes of the prosecutor, she gazed back at me and said, "No questions, your honor."

At this point, the judge looked over all the evidence she had before her, taking her time to evaluate each and every document. She looked in the direction of my attorney, myself and then to the prosecutors and uttered the words I'd been longing to hear, "This case is set for a jury trial". That is exactly what I wanted; I wanted the opportunity for all the evidence to be viewed in a court of law.

I left court that day and returned home, hoping that we could prepare for the future. The future did not turn out quite as I thought it would be.

Libertad

Life goes on. I still had my fair share of challenges. One of the concerns of my family and friends was that I would write this book. They pleaded with me to stop, to forget the past, to just go back to lounging in my pool and planting flowers. That's not who I am. I am Celia Belt, a burn survivor, abuse survivor, and the survivor of a near-fatal accident that nearly took my life. I fear

Left: As my Jacket Reads- Freedom- Libertad!

nothing. Let them retaliate, let them hate, I know I have the love of family and friends. I will stand my ground. I know my truth, and I am sharing it on these pages.

With all the support Venomara provided, I was eternally grateful. My daughter, equally supportive, also wanted me to just be a mom and Mimi to my grandson. I can be all those things, but I will never stop fighting for my rights, my civil liberties, and my rights as a disabled American citizen. More importantly, I am here for the rights of others, for those that go unheard.

I did my best to resume life as I knew it and remained true to the new restrictions placed on me by the court system. I was dealing with a large dose of P.T.S.D. I was no longer able to hug my daughter or to have anyone touch me in even the slightest of ways. I had experienced, on two occasions, in my own home, been manhandled by very large police officers. People I should have trusted, people I had called for help, and had brought nothing but harm. A piece of me was shattered. Somewhere deep down within, I was unable to be touched, unable to trust, I'd need help healing from these wounds. Thankfully, I was taking some medication, non-narcotic, that helped with the bad dreams that accompany someone who has experienced the trauma I had gone through. I was determined to get through this if it killed me. I thought back to working with Soldiers returning from war, the ravages they had seen, how many returned broken and beaten, and the support I offered them, now, it was me that required that support. I could do this, I must.

Living on house arrest has its challenges. I was not allowed to leave my home or yard. I could only go to doctors' appointments with the permission of pretrial, and I had to bring in notes from doctors following each visit. If I had an emergency, if Bobo the Cat needed to be taken to the vet, I would be unable to take him. It's an awful way to live, but these are the cards dealt to me. I must play with them.

With my fearless self, I move forward. I face a trial. I am fearless, I am whole, I know my truth, I have by my side good attorneys, and I have the backing of the advocates of Texas Disabilities and Texas Jail House Project. I also have family and friends. They fear for my life, my future, and my state of mind. I fear for NOTHING. What more can they do to me? BEAT me again... They have already done that... IMPRISON me...They have already done that... Take away my CIVIL RIGHTS... Trounce on my right to U.S. AMENDMENTS... They have already done that... They have done that... FALSELY ACCUSE me... They have done that... I STAND... I AM... Celia Belt...

On the twenty-fourth of May, I was feeling fearless. I rang the local police department and kindly asked if I might be granted just one of my phones back. The one that was my direct link to burn survivors around the world, and also the phone that would help me reconnect all my accounts. Without it, I was at a loss. I was exact...I could not believe what I was hearing... when they returned my call and informed me that I would be granted not only my three phones but also my driver's license. I have no idea why this sudden shift happened. I was simply thankful.

I was able to open all three of the phones and view that my photos, videos, phone calls and texts had all been downloaded. However, this didn't get me anywhere, although I had my phones, the access codes had been changed and AT&T would no longer grant me access. So I was stuck, once again. There was nothing I could do.

I decided to take this one step further. I inquired about the retrieval of my guns. A hot button for sure, yet one I had to address. I received no response. A few days later, I received my second letter from Attorney General Ken Paxton's office. I had already received one letter from his office denying me and my attorney's right to view the bodycam video of my arrest. Interestingly, it named my daughter-in-law, Betty, as wanting a copy of the same report. Attorney General Ken Paxton's office, once again, was denying access to the bodycam footage that we had requested. I might add that at the time I was sending letters and receiving responses from the attorney general's office, he was being impeached by none other than the Governor of Texas, Greg Abbott. I met Greg and his lovely wife, Cecilia. First, at an awards presentation, at which time I was given the Governor's Award, and then secondly, on the burn unit at B.A.M.C. Greg sustained burns, and I was charged with keeping the media away, protecting him and his family from any intrusions. I have great respect for him and enjoy the company of both him and his wife.

Venomara had sent her crew over to the house to help me. I had known them for years, and it was good to see them again. Mo and Jorge helped me place several of my furnishings and my treasured art collection back into the house. All had been packed away in preparation for the home's renovation. It's tough to describe, but I felt the exuberance as each lovely piece of furnishings was restored to its original place. To say nothing of the hanging of a portion of my beloved art collection. I was once again surrounded by the works of Theo Tabiosse, Rex Hausmann, Anna Carl, and so many more.

Unpacking my collection of books brought back a tidal wave of memories. I can remember each and every place where I purchased those books, my art, and the loved ones by my side. Framed photos of my loved ones appeared, and I was reminded of the love I bore for them. As Mo and Jorge packed up to leave, I realized I had nothing to offer them in the way of a tip. What I did have was a Moonlight Fund coin. Coining in the military is a solemn and honored privilege. I took that coin and handed it to Jorge. In military fashion, I turned his hand upside down and placed the coin in his hand. This was my tip.

The next few days I spent time sorting through family memories, my treasured keepsakes of time gone by. I reveled in the unveiling of each new piece of art. For each represented a time in my history, a love, a cherished memory. A new moment opened with each box, a loving memory, a treasured friend, or a beloved family member.

I rang my personal doctor, Dr. V. I wanted to thank her for the careful care she had provided me with during such a stressful time. It was like balm to my soul to hear her voice again. I simply wanted to say thank you. She was kind and I know, in my soul, she is still there to watch over me.

Life at home was different. I had little access to my assets, my credit had been plundered, and I was dealing with a wreck of a house. Hillary arranged for me to receive food from the local food bank, Hill Country Bread. This was not only humbling, but it was also demoralizing. Yet, I had to accept their help and be thankful for it. For the first time in months, I had access to fruit and vegetables. It matters not that they were canned; they were mine, and my body desperately needed them. I viewed my home, and it was quite a mess. Hillary and her friends had helped themselves to the pool and my kitchen. The sink was filled with dirty dishes, flies abounded, and the pool was a mess of children's life jackets and play accessories. I do not fault Hillary; she was raised with a full-time nanny, a six-day-a-week maid, and me, the ever-cleanly mother picking up after her. It was just a part of the process. I needed to clean up. She had also just gone through an extremely difficult experience. Her mother had been in jail. What that must have done to this poor girl, I can only imagine. She shared with me these words, "Mother, it wasn't just you in that isolation cell; it was me also."

I gave some thought to exactly how I was going to regroup without filing suit against those who had wronged me. What recourse did I have available to me? Those involved had no assets. I had also given my word to my soul that I would forgive all involved. Yet, I was in a hurting way. I was accepting food from a food bank, I owed the credit company and banks money that Ahlab had charged, and I needed to replace my service dog. I had no other option than to ring State Farm and make a claim. I was honest with them. I now had evidence: the witness' in two states who saw Ahlab with my stolen property and a witness' who had key information regarding the theft of my dog. I explained the entire sordid story, which must have seemed farfetched, to say the least, but it is the truth. I had never been late with a payment and was a long-standing good customer of State Farm. I was a victim, and I had suffered a loss. I knew I could not claim Taboo. I assumed I could claim Risqué and the property Ahlab had taken. I now had proof of the property she'd taken.

It was a frustrating and tedious process, and I still don't know how or if it's going to work out. I must simply forge forward with the hope that all will work out in the end. My agent was caring and disgusted by what had happened to me. They handled my claim and, for several months, did all they could to work with the local police to subrogate the claim. I had made a police report regarding the theft; I also provided the police with a list of witnesses and their phone numbers; regardless of this, the report was closed. This made subjugation difficult for State Farm. It would be sixteen months before my insurance company would tolerate any more, and once they had gathered enough evidence, they would take matters into their own hands.

With my ever-clever cat, Bobo the Cat, and yes, that is his full name. I never imagined a cat could bring so much comfort. Bobo the Cat came into my life back in 2015. I was battling scorpions and rats out at the ranch. During one of Randy's calls home, I asked if I might acquire a cat. He agreed, and Hillary sent me to a local cat adoption; she had previously worked with them and found her beloved Haku, a Turkish Angora with the most amazing eyes. He had one of each, blue and green. She adored him.

I was equally as lucky. I picked a baby out of a litter of four, thinking they were Siamese with some sort of deformity due to them having bobbed tails. I would later discover, through some digging and checking with breeders, that I had no Siamese on my hands. What I did have was a Mekong Bobtail. An interesting breed, this bred cat is most like a dog. He was quite the hunter. I never had problems with snakes, scorpions, or rats once Bobo the Cat came on board. The feral cats that plagued my property disappeared. I'm not sure if Bobo the Cat shied them off or if he may have eaten them. I viewed him taking on wild animals much larger than he. During Randy's last days, I was sitting with him, reminiscing about our life together, when in the window, the outline of two animals appeared. This was accompanied by a loud screech, a call I had not heard since my childhood in Wisconsin. I quickly grabbed Randy's flashlight and bolted out the front door.

What I saw was amazing. The two outlines I saw were of Bobo the Cat and a full-grown badger. Bobo the Cat stood his ground; the badger was emitting that scream while Bobo the Cat remained silent. On another occasion, I had a large rattlesnake that took up residence in my horse barn. I had seen him and his shed on several occasions, but I was unsuccessful in finding his exact hiding spot. Enter Bobo the Cat. I called Bobo the Cat out to the barn one morning. On this day, the snake was curled up next to my hay, just adjacent to my Friesians' box stall. I turned both of my horses out and my miniature Sicilian Donkey, Lilly. What happened next was amazing to watch. I could have easily grabbed a gun or a rake and dealt with this; instead, I watched as Bobo the Cat chased the snake down my long drive and out into the road.

I didn't see Bobo the Cat for the rest of the day. I had no idea if he lay dead of a rattlesnake bite or if he was simply out hunting. He appeared that evening, no worse for the wear, and quickly curled up with my German Shepherd, Taboo. It was heartening to watch as Taboo licked Bobo the Cat's fur and tenderly gave him a nudge of his nose. I've not seen a cat and dog quite as close as these two. They were buddies from the day I introduced this small kitten to my large German Shepherd. It was truly something to behold.

Just two short weeks home, out of jail, happy and humbled to be home with my cat and the creature comforts of life, I lost Bobo the Cat. He was breathing heavily, and, on a Saturday, he was lying under my bed. Kodey had been over earlier in the day and had mentioned the need for Bobo the Cat to be seen by a veterinarian. I agreed, and I reminded him, nonetheless, that I was under house arrest and if he could please take him in on Monday. Within minutes of Kodey's departure, Bobo the Cat let out a scream, several in fact. I had never heard him emit such sounds. My dog Charlie responded by lying under the bed with him. I knew I had to get Bobo the Cat in with the emergency vet and fast. I rang Kodey; he was at my home within moments as I spoke with the clinic and confirmed they had oxygen on hand.

What happened next, as I watched Kodey move slowly from under the bed with my sweet Bobo the Cat in his arms, was heartbreaking. In the kindest of voices, Kodey said, "Celia, I think he's gone." I looked down at Bobo the Cat, and he lay lifeless. It was at this point that my dog, Charlie, lay down beside him. A fitting farewell for such a groovy cat. There was no time for tears. I was still on the phone with the vet's office, and they had overheard everything. I kindly thanked them for their time and wrapped Bobo the Cat in my arms. His warm body, his kind soul, and his fearlessness were all still there, but he wasn't. Kodey and I took him out to the backyard for burial. I scoured the garage for a good shovel. Knowing that Charlie may dig him up, I made the decision to bury him in the vegetable garden I had given to my grandson on his fourth birthday. I knew he'd enjoy the labor of planting the seeds and checking their progress each time he visited me. Doing so meant I would need to unearth the radishes, onions, and flowers that were already appearing. I removed all, and once I felt I was deep enough, I lovingly placed Bobo the Cat on the soft earth, his new home. I covered him with fresh dirt and replaced the vegetables and flowers. How fitting that he should rest there, in a box built for a little boy to watch and enjoy the fruits of his labor. Just three days prior to this, my daughter Hillary lost her Turkish Angora, her Haku. I can still see Haku climbing the century-old oaks at my ranch as an amused Bobo the Cat looked on. I guess they are together, scaling some new trees in a land far, far away.

Once I arose beyond the noise and confusion, I knew my path. All those that had come against me... I was determined I would not find a way through the legal system and the family courts to bring everyone to justice. Let them go. Allow them to be free, perhaps one day they will develop a conscience. All of those who had betrayed me, the system that is so inept, and every single last one of them. They would enjoy the Karma that only this life can provide. They can beat me, they can jail me, they can demean me... But...they will never take away my dignity. My mind is clear, my thoughts consistent. I decided to offer forgiveness to all. It is not up to me to seek justice; that is for the Gods to decide.

Here again, I'm reminded of my promise of forgiving everyone. I could not pick and choose whom to forgive. Many of these people simply thought they were doing their job; others, well, the others, had motives I cannot comprehend. In the end, they will all be forgiven. Each of us has a contract on this earth, some to do evil, others good, we don’t choose, we are chosen.

Charlie Pickles

Just weeks into my second stay in jail, Hillary mentioned the need for me to move on and acquire a new dog. This was unthinkable to me. How could I possibly replace the love, protection, and respect I had with Taboo and Risqué. She visited a local pet rescue, stating they had two young hybrid German Shepherds for adoption. I told her to spend some time with them and let me know.

Above: Charlie, my four legged friend, during these dark days.

I wasn't ready for this, but I thought it might provide a good diversion for her during my incarceration. I was surprised when we next spoke that she informed me the two she had mentioned would not be a good fit, but there was another dog, a Great Pyrenees/German Shepherd cross, that seemed perfect for me. She mentioned that this particular dog loved to swim, and of course, I currently live in a home with a pool. It also brought back memories of swimming Taboo and Risqué in the river at the Bandera place. I told her to go ahead with the application process, and we would see from there. My dog training experience began with a Great Pyrenees breeder, and of course, I had extensive knowledge of German shepherds. As luck would have it, she was approved. She had shared with them that the dog would be placed with me once I was released and that I had a large yard and pool.

As luck would have it, I didn't return home as I thought. My court hearing was traumatic, and I was held on a "no bond" once again. This would force Hillary to keep Charlie at her apartment. I listened to her share her "Charlie" stories and how he was adjusting to life with my rambunctious three-year-old grandson. I knew it could not be easy; she desperately wanted to replace dogs in my life. I fought the idea, yet I was growing fonder of Charlie by the day. Hillary sent me a few photos of him, and my heart began to turn. The thought of returning home to a dog, even the thought of returning home offered a glimmer of hope to me. However, I still denied him staying with me once I returned home. As fate would seal the deal, I spent a few days with this incredible creature and quickly developed a love for him. It was obvious to me that he had some wolf cross in him. I had experience with wolves and understood that his training needed to be adjusted, and I took everything into consideration. I also knew that both my grandson and my daughter had developed a fondness for this animal; keeping him would be a bond and allow me the opportunity to show my gratitude. I love this dog. He provides companionship and a level of protection that I so desperately need at this time in my life.

When Hillary first picked Charlie up, she asked my grandson what his name should be. Interestingly enough, he chose the name "Charlie". I had originally chosen the name Charleston for Hillary so many moons ago and was thinking of Charlie for short. I found it cute that we now have a dog named such. My grandson chose a last name, Pickles. I ran a pickle company, VanHoltens, when Hillary was young. Another coincidence for sure. So... Charlie Pickles it was. He became a part of our life, like it or not.

I began training the young Charlie, taking into account his wolf content and his Great Pyrenees breeding; both are independent breeds and require specialized training. He responded well. He's extraordinarily bright, intuitive, and well-mannered. He's not very fond of men; he does, however, love Kodey, which is a good thing. I must admit here I love this dog. After years of importing high-end German Shepherds from the Czech Republic, Z.Lintichu's at that, I am humbled by this mutt of mine. I am grateful for his companionship and pleased by his presence.

Slammer Time

As I ponder my time in jail, I must reflect on all the good lessons learned, the hearty laughs, the tears, and the anguish shared by many. I don't need a fast car, I need no part of wonderful...I am wonderful, as are many of those people I have met during my incarceration. As I inked the deal on my next book, *My ValHalla*...much of the proceeds will benefit those less fortunate. I have three nonprofits in mind in different areas of the country. All serve burn survivors and wounded military members, causes close to my heart. As I move forward with this new life of mine, I often remember the lessons I learned in jail and the most practical things I learned. I now know how to feed several people with just one small bag of beans bought through the commissary. Mix the beans with what little meat was left on someone's tray, add a dash of Sriracha, which is also purchased with commissary dollars, and voila, you have a meal.

I also put my Jolly Ranchers candy to good use. I would hold them under a mildly hot shower and fill the room with the sweet fragrance of green apples and watermelon. I used a mixture of coffee and hair tonic for black people's hair, which contained vitamin E and a healthy dose of my Voltarin anti-inflammatory cream. I used this mixture of products on my badly swollen ankles. I have no idea if it helped. I had no other recourse, so I enjoyed the good soaking my new tonic offered me. I learned about the importance of using as little toilet tissue as possible. I learned to save my resources.

I learned other things, like how important family and friends are. To hear the voices of family and friends on the phone meant the world to me. I know it was an effort for them, those phone calls, to remain calm and comforting, when all they truly

Photo taken during a storm, I now find myself in a very different type of storm

wanted to do was break down and cry. I also developed a high regard for the guards. They may have been cruel at times, yet I came to realize they were simply doing their jobs, and it's not an easy task, dealing with inmates day after day. I got a sense that they were all overworked and underpaid. I will not place their names here, as I know each one by name. I hope they know that I respect them. Those long months spent in solitary confinement, when that door would open for meds or to use the kiosk, were like fresh water in a desert. I found myself looking forward to any human contact. I also appreciated Nurse Mac, as I'll call her. She was one tough cookie. It could not have been easy caring for me with my host of medical issues, yet she did. I know I drove her crazy with all my shenanigans. It was my sense of humor that kept me alive during those dark days, and I indulged in a healthy dose of it.

I busied myself each day with keeping my cell tidy, organizing it and cleaning. It was filthy when I was moved to this dark, small cell. I had nothing to clean it with, so, I wadded toilet paper into tight wads and used water and shampoo to clean the badly stained toilet and shower, scrubbing the floor and wiping the floor. Weeks later, I would be offered a cleaning bucket, mop and a rag, I was grateful for the opportunity to clean my new surroundings properly. The guards would remark that they had never seen the place so clean. I knew this would be my “home” for quite some time, I may as well make the best of it.

I organized my toiletries, books, and my food and made the most of it. I had to take pride in what little I had. I felt some sense of achievement each day as I cleaned and organized my abode, it also made the time pass. Time, there was always that to deal with, I had to find ways to pass the time, to not lose my mind, to keep my spirits up, both for myself and those I loved. This place, I would survive. With little diversions, hour by hour, day by day. I could not let the darkness, or the walls envelope me.

I pleaded with the guards to please, leave the three inch by twelve inch window open, that would allow me a bit of light to read, they never honored this request, I was left in the dark. The lights came on at 4:30 A.M., at which time a barely there breakfast was thrust through the metal hole in the door. Most mornings I kindly said, no thanks, not today and the metal would clang shut. The bright fluorescent lights remained on until 10:30 P.M., then I was left in total darkness. I longed to continue reading my books, or coloring. There was nothing to do, but lay there and listen to the guards in the nearby station or the inmate going through the throes of detox in the cell next to mine. I'd make a vain attempt to sleep, every fifteen minutes the metal door to the window would be opened for the guard to do his check, with a loud bang, it would open and be closed shut.. My eyes remained open, waiting and looking. Each night, crickets would appear from the drains in the floor, I guess they were also prisoners here, unable to escape. I was happy for their company. I would set out crumbs of food for them, hoping it gave them some sustenance. Their chirps were welcome songs on these long nights of mine.

My love of reading had returned to me in those days. I had not read a book since my accident. This was due in part to the vertigo I experienced and continue to live with. My mind also did not work the same. I found it difficult to barrel through a five-hundred-page book the way I used to. My treasured collection of books had been packed away. Yet, in that cold and dark room, I rediscovered my love of reading. Hillary made excellent choices on Amazon and kept me well-stocked on reading material. I spent hours in that bed, getting lost between the pages of one extraordinary book after another. When I wasn't reading, I was coloring. Once again, my daughter made some good choices here, choosing coloring books that were not only difficult in technique but also awe-inspiring. By the time I left, I had purchased six sets of colored pencils through the commissary. They only offered twelve colors, I grew quite adept at blending the colors with water and several different elements to create different textures and colors. I loved creating my little works of art and soon realized I could also purchase stamped envelopes. It didn't take long for me to begin sending my finished works of art to my daughter, grandson, and my friends, Tink, Jimmy, and Venomara. I loved putting my mail out under the crack in my door. Knowing it would soon be collected and routed to those I loved. These people had all done so much for me, and I knew they were worried sick about my time in jail. It was a simple gesture and all I had afforded to me during this time. I hope I brought a smile to their faces and gave them some little glimmer of hope. I would be coming home soon, perhaps not as soon as I had hoped, but someday I'd be home.

Abode

As I settled into life back at the Belt Abode, I pondered my children, how they were raised, and the achievements each has made in their adult lives. Justin, my eldest, was the father of one child. His son has autism, and Justin has handled this beautifully. He's quite successful and a good provider, and he is his own person. He's the true badass of my three children. He does, however, possess a weak link, and that is he married a loser. Bethany, his wife, or Betty as she is called, lost her first child to C.P.S. custody. Her mother was awarded custody of her daughter, and Betty has never seen the child. Betty has some serious mental health issues and Justin feels compelled to care for her.

Sunset at my home, how I longed for home, to see the sky again!

Desperate to have a child, she talked Justin into allowing her to become pregnant. Justin did not want children, yet he acquiesced, and she gave birth to a son. I purchased a lovely home for them and gave them an additional one hundred thousand dollars to pay off their debts. I couldn't bear the thought of them returning home from the hospital with their son, to a rented home with such staggering debts. With one condition, they repay half of the one hundred K back. The home was theirs to keep; they simply needed to make payments of fifty thousand dollars. Betty convinced my son that the fifty thousand did not need to be repaid, and I never saw a dime of it. Wouldn't you know, I raised him, he's a spoiled entitled human being. I have myself to blame for his selfish, self-centered behavior.

Jarred, my second-born, is married to a charming and brilliant girl. He met Vanessa several years back, and they enjoyed a long courtship. I couldn't be more pleased with not only his taste in women but also his remarkable business achievements. I raised him in a business environment; he saw me run companies, develop real estate projects, found a nonprofit, and go on to be a public speaker and author. Jarred certainly inherited my sense of business, for he is incredibly successful. I had my youngest child, Hillary, on my own and raised her alone. You never know how that's going to work out. I had the help of nannies. I also had the support of my ex-husband, David, and his wife, Peggy. They were the only people who supported my decision to keep this child back in 1992, in a time when being an unwed mother was not the most popular of things to be, much less an unwed, successful businesswoman. Even my mother was against me having a child on my own, she feared it would jeopardize my career. Hillary is, well, nothing less than remarkable. She is the perfect combination of her father, Greg

Swindell, and me. She made the decision to study for her master's in developmental psychology, and with the help of my ex, D.J., she has fared well. All with raising a young child on her own. Oh, how history repeats itself. She is my true champion, and I would not be alive and well without her loving support.

I raised them to believe in themselves. I also raised them to have wings. Wings to fly on their own. To leave the nest, to be their own person. I instilled values in each of them: be the best version of yourself each and every day, and live your own truth, for that is all you've got. I also, or at least I hope, raised them to believe in the value of their words. Never lie, don't cheat your fellow man, and always, always care for your siblings. I'm proud I completed that part of my life. Now, I am on to influence the next generation, my grandson.

As time progressed, I dove even deeper into the damage done by my cousin, Ahlab. I was facing not only identity and asset theft, the looting of my home and my property, but my credit rating had also tanked. From a nice level of eight hundred plus, it was now reduced to a mere four hundred and three. I placed a fraud alert too late. Hillary suggested at one point that I cut my losses and file for bankruptcy. This was unthinkable. I was raised by my mother, her name was also Celia. She was a businesswoman and lived by the truth. She was not only a staunch Nordic, a Viking, but she was also an accountant. The ethics she bore into this soul of mine will last this lifetime, and I would never, ever file and give others the burden of my situation. I would somehow find a way around this situation and pay everyone for what had happened to me. I had to take ownership. I opened a door that should have been shut. I loved, trusted, and valued the wrong people, and in the end, the fault lies with me.

I reached out to several advocacy groups, hoping against hope that there was some help. The answer was always the same; unless I pressed charges against Ahlab and Tubbs, I was tough out of luck. The practicality of pursuing them was dauntless. They had no assets to seize, and, in this case, I would be taking my daughter's advice: "Allow Karma to take care of these things." Good advice from my thirty-year-old youngest child and advice that I have taken to heart. Some people are not worth our time, our energy, or our hard-earned resources. With this in mind, I once again pulled up my bootstraps and readied myself for the next ride in this wild life of mine. I'd survive this, I had to; there was simply no other choice.

I was on fire, fire to survive, to ensure my safety, forgive those who betrayed me, and move forward. I believe in dreams; as a young girl, I would sit on my porch and dream. Each and every one of those dreams came true. Is it Manifest Destiny? I'm unsure. What I am sure of is that I am grateful, I am humbled, and I am whole. You may view me as weak, perhaps fragile, or less than humble. In the end, I am me, just me, and for that, I am grateful. It's quite simply, all I've got to work with.

As I was typing these words, a seizure hit a full-blown, grand-mal seizure. I had not had one since the night I was arrested. I'd been compliant, taking my meds in jail, Nurse Mac made sure of that; now, at home and alone, I was suffering. Trying to get back, stop the shaking, and place the mouse in my hands. It was of no use. I continued to flail about, unable to control even the slightest of my body's contortions. I was once again a prisoner in my own body. I looked up at the screen and saw what had been typed... line upon line of only those keys I could reach. The z's and a's were endless. I begged to be brought out of this nightmare. I begged, and I begged. I was making an endless attempt to keep writing, knowing these might be my last words. The last words my children might read, the last words the world would hear from me, I had to keep going, but all I could do was slam the keyboard, slam and slam with uncoordinated fists.

The room became silent. I wished Taboo and Risqué were here, and I needed my service dog by my side. Charlie was not ready for this; he was not yet trained, nor was he prepared to witness such an event. The silence in the room was deafening yet the noise in my head was terrifying.

Once the seizure subsided and I could make my way to the phone, I rang Venomara. Her kind voice responded, reminding me to take my anti-seizure drugs and my hydroxyzine. I avoid any benzodiazepines. Just days before, I met with my doctors. Their concerns were real, and they ordered home health care to monitor my drugs, in addition they ordered home health care to access if I needed any help with cooking and cleaning. I didn't require help with the home. I did, however, need help with my medications. How I wish that referral would have taken place in the week. I learned a valuable lesson, at all costs, whatever it takes, whatever system worked in the past, I must take my medication as prescribed. My life depended on it; home health care would not always be here. Kodey would not always be here; at times, I would need to depend on me.

My current suffering is nothing compared to losing the five people that meant the most to me. I can still feel them, each and every one of them. My grandmother Iris, gone at age fifty-four, my aunt Rhonda, killed at age twenty-four, my mother Celia crossed over when she was seventy-two, her daughter and my sister Audra left us at age forty-one, and my Randy, my beloved husband, crossed over at age seventy. They watch over me in a way that is tough to describe yet easy to accept. I am many times told that the "average" time to mourn the loss of a husband is X... well, there was nothing average about the love I bore for Randy, and there is nothing average about the way I miss him. It wasn't a perfect marriage. No marriage is. Will I love again? Yes. When the time is right, until that time, I remain Celia Belt.

My Trynattee

On Monday, June 6, I was standing with Kodey in my kitchen, going over a list of tasks to be completed when I looked down at the phone. I was ecstatic to have Kodey back in my life. He is much more than a bodyguard; he is my "soulguard." The new security system he installed in my home is directly linked to his phone, and I want it that way. I feel safe and looked after. Should anyone assault me in my home again, I know it will be seen and recorded, and I will be saved. As I got to the phone call, it read... State of Illinois. Could this call be about my cherished niece, Trynattee? I'd been worried sick about her, knowing she'd been in the hands of my cousin, Ahlab.

I answered the phone, and a woman introduced herself as Michelle, an investigator with the State of Illinois. Yes, it was regarding my niece. My first words were... "Is she safe?" Her response was swift and reassuring. She went on to tell me that Trynn had been placed with Rick, her stepfather. Rick came into Trynn's life at an early age; she had lost her father in a car crash and was being raised alone by my baby sister, Audra. Rick is one of those fine, upstanding Midwestern type of guys, and just like me, he lost the love of his life, my sister, Audra, in 2017. I was both relieved and elated that Trynn was in his loving care. Not only was she back in her childhood home, a home that had originally belonged to my mother, then by my sister, but her room had remained untouched. She found it exactly as she had left it. She was now safe.

Michelle went on to share as much as she could with me. Ahlab had placed Trynn in a mental hospital for three months. She did so once Trynn had disclosed to her school counselor that Ahlab's son, Brute, had raped her four times. Ahlab had custody of Trynn; this proved to be quite a problem for the state. When Ahlab picked Trynn up from the state mental hospital after months of incarceration, she filed a protective order, basically leaving my fifteen-year-old niece out on the streets. A horrifying thought for any of us to fathom. Michelle scrambled to find adequate housing for Trynn; nothing was available for a child who had undergone recent abuse. It was only through Michelle's resourceful nature that Trynn was placed with Rick. A kind act for which I will forever be grateful.

As our conversation progressed, she went on to tell me that Ahlab showed up to meetings with state investigators with Louis Vuitton bags. I described the bags, and sure enough, they were all bags that had been in my closet. All were taken during the time Ahlab had looted my home. More importantly, she shared with me that she had an uneasy feeling about Ahlab and her motives. Ahlab was collecting social security checks from the deaths of both Trynn's parents. She may have also doubled down on this and received free health care for her own children once she adopted Trynn. A large web she had weaved.

Michelle informed me there was much she could not share. I would need to speak with Trynn directly. She shared Trynn's number, and I immediately rang her. I was elated to hear her voice. The sweet cadence of her voice, the confidence exuded there, and the remembrance of my sister was sweeping.

What she shared with me tore at my soul; I wanted to punch the wall, but thankfully, I didn't. Trynn had been raped four times by Ahlab's son Brute, in addition to other atrocities. She also shared with me that Christmas had been "over the top," with Ahlab gifting everyone with expensive gifts that they had no idea where or how she could have come about acquiring. I knew immediately that these were items she had taken from my home. I felt rage and anger beyond belief. I could care less about the items Ahlab had stolen from me; I was heartbroken regarding my niece, her rape, and the abuse she received at the hands of Ahlab and her son, Brute. I allowed her time to talk before broaching the subject of counseling. She mentioned that help was on its way and that she was more than eager to begin the process.

She also shared that she was currently in the care of her stepfather, Rick. I was relieved to hear this. This was the dying wish of my sister that Trynn would be allowed to live with her stepfather. My greatest hope had been realized: my baby sister's daughter had been rescued. My promises to Audra had been honored; Trynn was now in the hands of Rick, in the way the Gods saw fit. She was safe, and that's all that mattered. I can only

Audra and her daughter, Tryn.

hope and pray that the years spent in Ahlab's care do not linger, that the nightmare of that abuse will somehow be repaired and forgotten.

In further conversations with Michelle, I shared my concern that Brute would not be fully prosecuted for his rape due to his age. We also discussed the fact that Ahlab, being the custodial parent, was, in fact, responsible for this crime. She had knowledge of the crime. The state had evidence. Trynn had taken evidence to her counselor at school, and the police had also done a search of Ahlab's home, at which time they uncovered more evidence. The deck of cards was falling. I could not and would not get involved. All I could do was sit back and wait and be supportive. I did, however, make resources available. I would and could hire the best attorneys in Chicago to avenge the injustice done to my niece. Karma would be done. I was reassured that the state of Illinois was investigating the case and knew that Ahlab had indeed hired an attorney to defend Brute and herself in this case. Perhaps there was justice, after all. I would keep a very close eye on all of this. I would defend the rights of Trynn, I would keep those promises I made to my sister, as she lay dying, I would always care for her daughter.

Le Misere'

I woke to a glorious Monday morning. The Texas sun was shining, and the pool beckoned me. Glorious streams of water, beckoning colors of green, gold and blue. As I poured my coffee and lit my cigar, I sat and viewed my expansive yard with Charlie by my side, thankful for all I had. I pondered my upcoming book deals. Which way should I go? With the big book publisher, or should I indie publish? I wasn't yet sure what would be the best route for this book; I was, nonetheless, sure the answer would be revealed to me. I had changed several of the names in the book, protecting myself from any future lawsuits and those in the book. Whether they were guilty parties or not, all deserved my protection.

Above: Moonlight Fund gala with wounded Soldiers Issac Gallegos, Shilo Harris, my daughter and I.

Then it happened, the phone rang. I answered and heard the ever-stern voice of Officer Moreno of the Kendall County Pretrial Department. She stated I was in violation of my pretrial conditions. She further went on to describe that I had left the property the Sunday before. I had not. I was at home the entire day. I was training Charlie. In fact, I had a massive grand-mal seizure on that day and had retired to bed. She continued to insist that I was in violation, even declaring the name of the street that I was located on. The street was the next one over to my home. This would make sense, as my property was an extra long lot that extended along that street.

She would not listen to me. I offered to have a drone shot taken of my home; again, she denied it. I contacted my attorney immediately and shared this information with him. As soon as Kodey arrived, we filmed the yard, and I sent the video to Officer Moreno. I CC'd my friend Venomara and my attorney Robert on this. The pretrial department and the DA's office were once again looking for any reason to rearrest me, just as they did before. This added stress and brought on a bout of seizures. I doubled down on my seizure meds, taking another dose, knowing it could be lethal. I was just a day away from my home health care nurse arriving, yet I had to do something. Taking additional doses of medications was my only recourse.

I shared this situation with my friend Jimmy during one of our early AM calls. We are both night owls, and I always count on him for late-night conversations. I had shared with him on several occasions that I planned on moving back to the Texas Hill Country. It was during this conversation that we began looking online at properties available with land in the Bandera area, and there it was. Rancho De Sol. Wow, it was perfect: a main house, a pool, a guest house, a horse barn, a party pavilion, and eight acres with stunning views of the hill country. Better yet, it was in my price range. It didn't take me long to contact the agent. I'd have to purchase this place sight unseen, as I was not allowed to travel, and I didn't want the local police to know where I was moving to. I'd send Kodey to have a look. I call this manifest destiny.

I desperately needed to remove myself from Boerne. I needed to get back to the Texas Hill Country. I required some form of safety in my life. I hesitantly set about my plan. Would the authorities allow me this? I was unsure.

As my discussions with state authorities in Illinois progressed and I learned more about the case against Ahlab, everything started to make sense. The local police were coming to my home not out of any intention to harass me; they were coming here at her request and the request of the attorney, Ned, to do "wellness checks." It became abusive, yes, but it was Ahlab, Trish, Tubbs, and Ned who initiated it. Ahab and Trish put me away in psych hospitals three times and eventually in jail on trumped-up, false charges.

I never threatened anyone online. That's not my style. I want nothing to do with these people. These are people who benefited from my largeness. I was kind to them, not only in terms of my time but also in terms of my resources; my money was theirs; that's the way I operated. I'm not a selfish person. If I have an issue with someone, I meet them head-on. I hired a good private investigator; it ended there. It hurt so bad to be betrayed; I had to put this mess into the hands of someone else. My hopes and dreams did not end, but the fight in me had been beaten out. I was quite honestly afraid of Ahlab and her crew; wouldn't you be? After all they had done to me. Literally, they took away months of my life, months of seeing my children, my grandson, and my friends. Months of helping burn survivors. Months of book signings and public speaking engagements. They took all that away from me, and I knew, somewhere deep in my heart, that we're not done yet.

I awoke on a Thursday morning, ready to face my pretrial meeting and my mandatory counseling that was scheduled to begin that A.M. To be honest, with what I'd just lived through, I could use some counseling, and if it was low cost, it was even better! I lay in bed thinking about my cousin, Keena. How I had adored her. She was like a Goddess to me. I wondered if she had a clue as to Ahlab's intentions regarding her own mother, my Aunt Dianne. I let my mind wander. What if I reached out to her, and what if I shared with her that not only had Ahlab stolen my identity, but she had seized my assets, my valuables, and my dogs and attempted to overtake my estate and my person? Should I share this with her? I decided I best wait until the investigators are further into their duties and I have full control of my identity, or perhaps I will wait until the day that Ahlab and Tubbs are held accountable for their actions. Do I look forward to that day? No, honestly, I do not. I don't know what the future holds, but I do know that all parties involved have committed numerous federal offenses. Will they be prosecuted? I don't know. I will not be the one to prosecute them; I will allow the system to work; if it works, then justice has been served; if it doesn't, well, there is justice in the heavens; of this, I am certain. As for me, I am tasked with surviving this nightmare, if only for one purpose, and that may be to share this story with others to ensure that it does not happen to them.

On a Thursday afternoon, Kodey was in one of his "moods." I gave him his space. He was, after all, a thirty-year-old and sometimes showed his immaturity. I needed a good "clean" of the house. I suspected the phones had been compromised. I was referred to a local private investigator. I rang him; we'll call him Joe. He answered immediately. We set up an appointment for the next morning. I cared for Kodey like a son. I wanted the best for him. I was not in a position to pay him his worth, and I shared this with him. My dream was to one day pay him his worth. He'd have to be a team player. He'd have to believe in that. If not, he'd not be a part of the team. I don't have a crystal ball. I have no idea what the future holds. I can only move forward with the best version of myself.

Hillary and Venomara, usually my biggest champions, had suddenly found it difficult to accept the new, independent version of me. The stronger, more independent version of me. They had for so long, cared for the broken me, that as I rose from the flames, and became the once strong woman that I had always been, they were fearful.

I had plenty of issues on my plate yet to deal with. I assumed my trial would be taking place in July. I was only recently told that it was only a "hearing." A hearing?! I wanted a trial. I had fought to pass a competency examination. I wanted a trial. I wanted the bodycam video to be revealed to the public, and I wanted this to end. The Attorney General of Texas's office, Ken Paxton's office, was still fighting to release the body cam footage, as was the city of Boerne. I had a right, by way of discovery, to that video. This was going to be a battle. I suspected that the DA would go for a plea deal, at which point the body cam would never be made public, and perhaps that is what will happen; I will accept that. I am in the hands of a very competent judge and in the hands of the Gods.

I contacted a security agency in San Antonio; we'll call them Joe. My first meeting with Joe exceeded all expectations. We met for two hours. We could have spent more time had he not needed to leave town. We discussed doing the "clean" of the home, my personal security, travel, some investigative work, and attending some meetings. Joe was likable, had a military background, and was married to someone in the medical field. I could not have asked for a better fit. His firm had the ability to offer all the services I would need on a go-forward basis.

Manifest Destiny

On a Thursday evening, I had a rather odd thing happen. One of the phones that Ahlab and Tubbs had corrupted and that I had shut down was lying on my desk. Why, I don't know. I looked down at it, and a message popped up from Bethany. I love her so much. She is my sister spirit. She ended our friendship last year. She needed to. I was toxic, and I knew it. It was painful living life without her, but I knew my drama didn't need to be hers. She needed to put her family first, and I needed to get my shit together. As I looked over her message, I viewed a plate full of oysters with a message that read "thinking of you." I'm unsure how old that message was. I instinctively replied, "This was a

Left: Bethany and I at my ranch.

phone that had been turned off with no service and no charge for nine months." She responded with, "Who is this?" Is that not wild? At times, we are given just the right, heartfelt message that buoys us, offers us a sign, a form of support, and a message of love.

This story gets better. The next message that popped up was from Carl. Years back we exchanged messages and he made a vain attempt to date me. As with all other men, I simply was not ready to date. The loss of Randy weighed heavy on this heart of mine. I knew that I was no ordinary widow, and that Randy would guide me in the right direction, when the moon rises west and the sun sets east.

I responded to Carl and received a quick response. My home phones were nonfunctioning, so it made it easy to carry on this conversation and limit our time to text only. We exchanged texts for nearly an hour before the home phone was once more functioning. Good timing, for sure. After having known him by text only for so many years, I found it was good to hear his voice and reconnect. He's a gentle giant, a kind soul. A dedicated family and a straight shooter. These are all things I can respect in a human being.

Life began to assume some steady rhythm. The scales of my life were balancing out, and after interviewing numerous publishers, I knew, in my heart, whom to publish *My ValHalla* with and to place the republishing of my first two books with. I have also begun work on my fourth book, *Libertad*, to be released in 2024. A more upbeat book full of inspiration, new adventures, and countries explored. I was certainly looking forward to writing *Libertad*. I had literally crawled my way back up and out of this mess. What a journey. Federal and state prosecutors were now taking a very close look at Ahlab and Tubbs.. It was much like a house of cards; it was all about to come crashing down on them. There was nothing for me to do. I didn't need to pursue damages. They would have plenty to deal with between my insurance company, State Farm investigating them and the authorities in numerous states.

I set up meetings with several of my new attorneys. I needed to add to my already solid base of legal representation, not only to protect myself in the future from people like the Ahlab and Tubbs of the world but also to set up the holding company and work with my security company. Whatever else they deemed fit we pursue, that was up to them. I hired the best, and I would take their advice. It felt so good to be free, or at least close to free again. I was still on house arrest. I had buyers for the Boerne home, was looking for another ranch in the Texas Hill Country, had money coming in, had a new book deal, and was preparing to meet Carl in person for the first time ever. We'd exchanged phone calls and emails for years. I simply wasn't ready to meet anyone. It's been nearly six years since Randy's death; perhaps it's time.

I am Nordic on my mother's side and Native American/ Irish on my father's. I cannot deny my blood. It runs through my veins like the night skies are dark and the days are light. It is this that keeps me strong, keeps me fighting the powers that be, those that would deny me my freedom and the basic rights that are granted to me as a U.S. citizen. It does not matter what my attorneys say. They fear for me, and offer sage advice. I will continue to fight on. I stand for what I believe in and for the basic freedoms provided for me by my forefathers all those years ago. This may all go on to some higher level; one day, perhaps this case and the crimes of those involved will be investigated or perhaps not. Perhaps it's a case for those that go unheard, for voices that are guided by the strong, by-laws that are quite simply abused by the power of those that feel they have the power to do so. For I am, at the end of the day, I am Celia Belt. I am nothing less and nothing more, just one voice.

It's a Friday

I had an extremely tough day. Pretrial did its best to derail me. They denied me access to meetings with my attorney, denied me meetings with my psychologist, and would not allow me to pay my fees, stating I could not stop to pick up the money order at my bank. At one point, I thought they would re-arrest me. I stood tall. What more could they do to me? They had already done it all. As Venomara and I entered their office, they refused Venomara's entry. That is a direct violation of A.D.A. Laws. She was with me due to my hearing loss and brain injury. We acquiesced. I was asked to go into an inner room with two of the officers. I could only guess what was about to take place. I very calmly began to take the documents out of my portfolio to produce proof of my appointments for that week. I made a vain attempt to apologize to the officer for any inconvenience I had caused them. Things got worse. They began a verbal attack on my service dog. All I could do was state he was ADA-approved and had documents in his vest from my doctor. He was medically necessary... Things were going downhill fast... very fast....

My mind reaches back to better memories; I remember that I always reserved the first-row center at every concert. Lynyrd Skynyrd was performing in town, and I purchased four tickets. I invited my friend Susan and her daughter to accompany Hillary and me. Little did I know that Hillary would attract the attention of Johnny, the former bass player of the Black Eye Peas. Well, as the story goes, Hillary resisted his advances and only had the best interests of the Moonlight Fund in mind. Several concerts later, many burn survivors enjoyed such concerts. Hillary achieved her goals, escorting numerous Soldiers to concerts, and Johnny, the over-amorous bass player, well, he never got his way with my daughter. Lesson learned. Don't fuck with us. We are here to serve those less fortunate. We are not here to serve ourselves. Hillary is a part of the Moonlight Fund; it is in her bones, in her blood. She is bound to this mission of ours and to all we serve, and I am proud of her.

My Hillary, always my Hillary, with me through thick and thin, threatened by my cousin and her padre, watched me sit in jail, raised a son alone, and sat back as I ran companies, founded a nonprofit, accepted awards, faced challenges, and forged through this life of mine. I wonder what it must be like to be her, to sit back and watch all of this. The pain and the suffering that it has caused her, the monsters that must stir in her closet due to being the daughter of Celia Belt. There is nothing I can do to change that. I was faced with similar challenges; my own mother was a stunning, gifted businesswoman. She sang like a bird, and her towering figure entering a room always stopped traffic.

I could never live up to that image; I was the little burned child, and I adored her. With this, I could relate to what Hillary must have gone through being my daughter. The difference between the two relationships was, however, profound; I built a solid foundation of love, trust, and devotion with Hillary. She knew that come hell or high water, I would always be there for her. I knew my mother loved me; she was so caught up in raising us, alone, on her own, with the responsibilities that entailed. In the end, I believe she did a great job, considering the deck of cards she was dealt.

I was beginning to feel a bit safer, and with that, I entertained a thought. Carl and I began having regular phone conversations, something I'd not had in the past with any man. I found a new freedom. The words flowed, and my heart began to open with this man, this giant of a man. Carl shared that he was seven feet five inches tall. That must have presented so many challenges in his life. An athlete who had dedicated his life to coaching numerous sports, a part time bodyguard, and a professional fighter. I must be honest. I grew fonder of him by the day. Had Randy brought him to me? Was I finally able to once again love? I wondered..., after nearly six years alone, if I was becoming quite fond of him. Carl was set to come to visit the following week. I found myself looking forward to his visit in more than one way. My body was becoming alive. I was a woman once again; feelings, electric, powerful animal emotions, and raw cravings were once more mine.

I even ventured upstairs, an area I had avoided since Ahlab's habitation, and made one of the spare beds up. I did this initially for Carl's daughter, anticipating she would be visiting soon, but then the thought stuck with me: we'd be making love in more than one place. I was making the bed for us. I was preparing a nest, a second bedroom for the two of us to remain tangled in one another's arms without abandon. I'd let him have his way with me in the master; that California king would call our names. Perhaps I'd hit the massage button as I lay under his great power, perhaps not. But we'd also be there in this second bed. What better way to rid the upstairs of such troubling energy, of Ahlab's sick and twisted presence, of the filth she had left behind, that I had long since cleaned and rid myself of. I gave away every bit of furniture, replaced all the flooring and had the home painted in an effort to rid myself of all memory of her. Perhaps we'd make sweet and passionate love in an area that was once tainted by my cousin and her posse. I found myself asking if this was real.

I was at a point where I didn't know who to trust anymore or what was real. The line between reality and terror was so blurred. I lived in a state of constant fear, fear of the police, fear of Ahlab, and fear of fear itself. Hiring Joe and his team would bring me some form of safety, and I badly needed that. I was one scared little lady. I struggled with this, my fearless nature was at war with this newfound fear that had been placed in my life. I also feared for my daughter's safety. Ahlab had threatened her and my grandson on more than one occasion. Hillary moved to a more secure location, farther away from Tubbs. I'd need to provide some security to her and my grandson. I'd do this at any cost. We did all this discreetly.

Venomara made a comment a few weeks back as we were discussing the damage caused by Ahlab and her posse. She said it's like a house of cards, that it would eventually all come tumbling down upon them, that I would simply have to "stomach" it, ride out the storm, and wait for Karma to take its place. I did just that. I sought no vengeance. I waited. I waited for the investigators in Illinois to take custody of my niece. I waited for my insurance company, State Farm, to conduct their investigation into the theft of my dog and the items stolen from my home by both Ahlab and Tubbs. They thought they had gotten away with all of it. They were wrong. It had taken ten long months, ten months of misery for me. I had to sit back and watch as my image, my good name, my credit, and my assets were stolen from me. They nearly stole my faith. I prayed for the end; it never seemed to come; there was always some new "surprise," a new element to this story, a new source of pain I must deal with. The end was out of my grasp. I'd have to wait for the house of cards to fold, and I was ready to sit back and watch it all happen.

Found

Early Monday morning, I rang the Boerne animal shelter and gave my luck one last shot. I spoke with Stephanie; she was extremely helpful and found that Risqué chip had been registered just weeks before with a national registry. I was over the moon with hope. I rang the number she gave me. Minutes turned into hours. When I finally got a person on the line, my heart sank, and I discovered it was one of the registers I had put into place. Another dead end. Things were heating up. State Farm Insurance had elevated their case to the investigative level and would soon be putting some heat on both Tubbs in Texas and Ahlab in Illinois. Both would be looking at grand theft charges. My private investigators were also preparing their case on both the grand larceny case of my missing dog and the grand theft of my property. I had just the week before contacted the Boerne police department and found they had dropped the case on both reports.

I reopened the case, only to find out they had once again dropped the case. Why on earth, would they continue to drop a case, one of which was a triple felony case? We would need to proceed without their help. It was becoming ominously obvious to me that local police were simply not on my team; in fact, they were doing all they could to entrap me, once again, as they had on so many occasions in the past. I once again dug deep for that survival chip of mine. As luck would have it, my beloved Aunt Betty rang me on that fateful Tuesday morning. She has been one of my truest angels. Since my early childhood, she offered words of hope and prayed with me. I also spoke with Venomara, Carl, and Joe, my private investigator, as we'll call him. In addition, I spoke with investigators from Illinois and Texas. My team was in place. I was not about to let local law enforcement intimidate me.

I was so ready to sign over the publishing rights of *Remarkably Intact* and *Silent Warrior* to my publisher, Marvin, and to seal the deal on this book, *My ValHalla*. I spoke with Marvin, and we agreed to the deal. I was moving forward, and it would take a freight train to stop me.

It's a Wednesday. Once again, I am required to check in with Officer Moreno at Kendall County Pretrial Services. I show up with all they require. I had to drive myself. As I slid into my new turbocharged Toyota, I noticed the fuel gauge showed five miles to empty. I mentioned this to Officer Moreno and asked if I might be allowed the extra time to stop and purchase gas, as the station is on my home. Her response was a swift NO... She went on to say that if I ran out of gas, I could call a tow company, have the car towed, and find my way home. Now, in anyone's book, does this make fucking sense?

I left my appointment under much stress, and as you would guess, I ran out of gas. I was close to a station and begged a few guys who were filling up to help me push the car in. We did so, and I was able to purchase some gas. Once home, I rang Officer Moreno and shared all that had happened. She simply said you were off course; you are out of your pretrial boundaries.

I had rung my daughter Hillary. My daughter was concerned about me breaking down on the road, with all my health conditions in one hundred plus heat. When she called Officer Moreno, she received an inappropriate response.... Moreno laughed at her.

I was home. I thought I was safe. Hillary burst through the door and began gathering up all valuables and making plans for Charlie Pickles,' our dog's, safekeeping. Pretrial had her so confused and afraid of my being arrested once again. They were using every bit of fear and intimidation during phone calls with my daughter. They were destroying our lives.

I did my best to comfort her, stating my bodyguard was on his way and my attorneys had been contacted. She went on to state her fears regarding Ahlab; she still had a will, an illegal one, but one nonetheless, that left my estate to her (Ahlab), not that Hillary cared or wanted my estate. She simply wanted me to know that it was a loose end I needed to clean up. She was in such a state of fear that I was soon to be arrested and that Ahlab would use this opportunity to once again attempt to seize my remaining assets.

I shared with Hillary that I had spoken with investigators from the state of Illinois, the investigators from the state of Texas, and the investigators of State Farm insurance just that day. That all was good. Soon, Ahlab and Tubbs will be investigated. It was all now in the hands of those much more powerful than me. That wasn't enough. She was still on edge, so I called one of my attorneys, and in her presence, I enunciated my need to have my will, advance directives, and trust revised. That seemed to calm her down.

My mind was reeling, why would they place so much damage upon the soul of this young, kind hearted young woman? Do they gain from placing such fear into the hearts of the innocent? What have they done to my family, and what damage have they wrought? The stress and deep-down fear that has been caused by all of this.

Days later, as I played in the pool with my much-adored grandson; the smiles and laughter were balms to my soul. I loved diving with him; Hillary always feared him diving at such a young age, but he did so fearlessly. I threw the dive rings into the deep end of the pool and dove the fourteen feet to retrieve them; he delighted in this, and then I would throw a few rings into the five-foot area for him, and off he would go for his own version of a deep dive. Our time was short. Hillary still fears the law and what they might do, so we must endure and accept this. She soon packed up and left. I had to understand that her fear was very real and that my time with both her and my grandson would be brief. I cherished each visit and prayed for the future, which is different from the reality we live in today.

Later that evening, I built a fire in the fire pit. As I sat back, listening to some Nora Jones, I stretched my legs out on the side of the pit, feeling the warmth. I looked up at the clouds and noticed them moving. The moon appears to flutter in between their grasp in a lover's dance. A storm was approaching, and it was my kind of evening. The clouds were leading me in the direction of love and lust, the trees, torn about by the wind, singing the song of torn street songs, begging out to me. Their branches reach in every complex direction, unsure of which wind to follow. And the fire burning in front of me, its flames, reaching high, then low, ever so sweet, and hot, beckoned from a time long ago when fear was not an ever-present part of my life. A time when laughter and love were the norm. It was all I could have asked for after this majorly fucked up day. I sat back, rolled my legs out, lit a cigar, grabbed my drink, and settled in for the ride.

I lived every day with the thought that the Boerne police had a key to my home. They had kept it during their raid while I was in custody. If they came through that door, I kept a gutting knife and my marlin spike by the bed. I lived in constant fear. I had no desire to harm a police officer; I grew up with police officers; my mother's best friend, Pauline, was a detective. She was a big part of our lives and I loved her dearly. I was raised to respect the authorities, not to fear them. Yet, this situation had reduced me to a place of fear, and I felt the need to protect myself. My mores had been twisted by what had been done to me, how could I respect those that had caused me so much harm? What is this world coming to? This situation Has destroyed my life, my daughter's life, my son's life, and that of my grandson, and dare I go on? I was a widow, living alone, in a place of total fear, fearing those that were paid to protect and serve. I struggled with these emotions. I know there are also very good, kind and protective police officers, those that take their oaths to heart. I prayed each night, prayed that I would sleep in a place of fearlessness, in a quiet field, where no one would touch me, or hurt me.

Why was I the target of so much hate? I was asked Why? So many people asked me that question... Why?

My day was filled with phone calls, investigators from the state of Illinois and Texas closing in on Tubbs and Ahlab. All good news, yet, all I longed for was to recover my dog. The money and the identity I had lost meant nothing; I simply wanted to find Risqué. I must admit, it was a comfort to hear that Tubbs and Ahlab would soon be under investigation... I rang my importer. It's time to import another dog, a Z.Lintichu. A male, he responded, there was a litter on the ground with a breeder in the Czech Republic, bred by the same German judge as had bred Taboo and Risqué I had imported with him in the past. This new pup would be named Karma Z.Lintichu. My Karma.

Once I got some cash under my belt, I set to the task of releasing all those held at the Kendall County Jail who could not, or simply did not have the funds to secure freedom... Libertad.... It would be theirs!!! I first set my sights on Angel. Although she was brutal to me, I knew in my heart she was a kindred spirit. A call to my bondsman, Megan, confirmed that after twenty-two months in jail, she had been released just a week after me. Then, I focused my attention on Emi, a poor soul unworthy of such brutal treatment. I was determined to make bond for Emi. She would be free. She would once again work at Denny's and enjoy all the laughter.

I remember, during my time in jail, Emi shared with me that she had pulled a knife on her mother during a psychotic episode. She was a grossly misunderstood human being and was treated quite badly in jail. It was obvious that she had a severe learning disability. She once looked at me during rec time, a plaintive look on her face. She said, "Celia Belt, will you forget about me once you're out and have your freedom? Will you forget about me?" The answer is ...No, I have not forgotten. I rang Megan, my ever-trusty bondsman, and found that Emi was still being held, and no one had stepped up to provide her bond. I was unable to free Emi for reasons I could not quite understand at the time. I had hoped to assist others entrapped by the system, but this would not come to pass.

My efforts to help those still in jail didn't work out. Angel had denied the bond and was sent to another facility. Emi's mother was granted guardianship of her, and that precluded anyone from issuing a bond and releasing her; this all made total sense and probably was good for me. I didn't need to be rescuing anyone but myself at the moment. I'd best be focusing my attention closer to home.

In retrospect of all that had taken place, the police were working off of poor knowledge. Ahlab, Tubbs, and Ned had been calling the police constantly, stating that I was not in the right state of mind. The police were simply acting on this misinformation. Events that took place due to their actions were unfortunate and extremely damaging, yet they couldn't be helped. Was I a victim? Yes. But in some odd way, so were the police. They were played, and they fell prey to a game that was being played out by Ahlab and her crew, their calls, their claims, and their insistent web of lies.

My finances were resurrecting themselves; little by little, I was gaining a foothold. I found amusement in the fact that during Ahlab's looting of my home and my safe, she overlooked Shakespeare's second folio. What a fool. She had no idea that that little book, alone, could have provided all the money she sought from me. Investigators from the State of Illinois, the State of Texas, and those from State Farm were closing in on Ahlab and Tubbs.

Karma was soon to have its due. I sought no vengeance. I forgave them all. I simply sat back and watched for the house of cards to fall. I secured a new contract on a pup from the Czech Republic, bred by the same German judge that had bred Taboo and Risqué. This new dog would be named Karma. How appropriate was that? I was close to signing the contracts for the republishing of my first two books, *Remarkably Intact* and *Silent Warrior*, and publishing this book, *My ValHalla*. All that was missing was, well, that one special thing. I believe in mermaids and dragons; I believe that shooting stars speak the language of love and that the streams carry our water to far-off people. I believe that nothing is by coincidence and that all comes our way by thought, deed, and trust. And tonight, I'll look at that one single star that calls out to me from the skies, and look back with my eyes of wisdom, my eyes of love, and my tear-stained face. I look into the firepit; I see my own eyes looking back; the journey endured... has all been worth it. My niece is now safe... if for nothing else. God... I endured so much... I would endure it for her...I survived...

Life is becoming complex. Venomara, my dear friend and my champion, has been diagnosed with cancer.

It's where the water flows... it's where the wind blows...and, that one seed grows...

Do I look forward to the day when I visit Ahlab and Tubbs are brought to justice? No, I don't care what happens to them... They may never be held accountable for their crimes, and I really don't care. I am free of them and the terror they brought to my life. My first speaking engagements will include what I experienced in the psych units. And in jail. Ahlab put me away four times, four times of agony... I will never forget... I met gang members, the Mexican mafia, mothers, sisters, and daughters. Many were falsely imprisoned in those hell holes. Why, oh why, did some eventually end up in the pen? Yes, many will. It's the system, and it's not fair; it just is. As with all things in this complicated world of ours, it's flawed, and on any given day, the wrong person can end up in the wrong place at the wrong time. Again, many of these people need to be here for crimes they committed. It happens. So yes, I'll speak at many venues soon. I hope to bring a message of hope, of kindness, of strength, and of survival.

I live by this quote: "Yesterday is already a dream and tomorrow but a vision. But today, well lived, makes every yesterday a dream of happiness and every tomorrow a vision of hope."

Never Ending

I thought I was done. I thought I had put this book to rest. Home on house arrest, waiting for trial. Yet, there were challenges ahead. Each week, pre-trail threatened to have me re-arrested. Tier relentless pursuit of me was something I'll never understand. One week, I stopped for gas on the way home from a doctor's appointment. I guess that wasn't allowed. The stress they were putting me through was beginning to show. With one look in the mirror, I could tell I was losing this battle. The lines on my face, the lack of color in my eyes, and the abuse were all starting to take their toll. The phone never stopped ringing, and the emails never stopped coming. Constant harassment was their calling card, and I was wearing thin. I spoke with my new private investigator, Kelly. He always had a way of calming me down. He assured me he was doing all he could to find attorneys to handle my case. A complex case it was, both from a criminal and civil standpoint. I spent countless hours on the phone with one of my D.A.R. friends, Dianne, on the phone. She had never given up looking for me when I had gone missing; she had also never given up looking for the dogs. She was such a source of comfort for me.

One night, as I was sitting by the fire pit, my thoughts drifted to Joan of Arc. It was not the flames that killed her at age fifteen; NO, It was the small minds of the small men that killed her. For she could outride, she could outhunt, outfight, outthink any one of those small men. It was the small men that killed her, not the flames. She never felt the heat, for in the end, it was them... those small men that felt the heat.

All I could do was continue to unpack and put the house back in order, swim, work out, and try to keep my head together. Placing my mind in a "good place" was paramount. Thankfully, I was in counseling and attempting to put the pieces of this shattered life back in order. Ahlab and her "crew" had done so much damage. I had some things to look forward to. I had ordered a new pup. Karma would be arriving from the Czech Republic in six weeks. He was a Z.Lintichu, the same lines as Taboo and Risqué. I was overjoyed at the thought of his arrival. I had his new bowls, blankets, toys, and food ready. I had found a scorpion in the house just weeks earlier and had added a pixie bob kitten, "Angel," to the household for insect control. My little family was coming together. Angel brought me a large amount of comfort during a very difficult time. This breed of cat, part wild, part tame is just what I needed to get through the long days and nights of stress and constant persecution and torment.

Then, it happened. I was sitting in my car, about to leave for my pretrial appointment, when a white S.U.V. approached my home and parked near my neighbors. I found it odd that no one exited the vehicle. I waited for a few moments. Then suddenly, three officers jumped out of the car, all wearing bulletproof vests and carrying heat. They approached my car and asked me to exit. I complied. They explained that they were there to search the home, and we went to the front of the house and entered. I asked if I could secure my cat first. She is, after all, just a kitten and wild, and I did not want to lose another animal in this mess I found myself in.

They asked if they would find anything in the home that would compromise me in any way, any weapons? I answered no, you have already taken all my weapons. I entered the home, secured Angel, and stood in the living room. They took my purse into the bedroom. I made an attempt to take it back. The three of them stood in my way. I pushed past them and took my purse. I stated I wanted to make a call to my attorney. They said I could make a call from the station. They continued to search the house. I was getting more and more frightened, and I knew I needed to call my attorney. My attorney was unavailable, so I called Kelly, my P.I. I stayed on the phone with me as they continued to search the house. At one point, they told me to open my safe. Kelly told me not to open it. My response was, "I have nothing to hide," so I opened it. They also found alcohol in the pantry. Although I am not on pretrial for any alcohol conviction. It is a condition of my pretrial that no alcohol is allowed in the home. I had only just recently allowed one of my wounded soldiers, Robbie, to stay at the home. I had also given Robbie quite a bit of money, and although Robbie did not drink, he had quite a bit of alcohol in the kitchen in preparation for his wife's birthday party. There was nothing I could do. I was in violation. I would have to take the hit for this. All the bottles were sealed. That made no difference. The officers took photos and left. I thought I was in the clear.

The next week, I was set to attend my pretrial meeting when my attorney, a new attorney I had just recently hired, informed me that I had an arrest warrant issued for me. I had just one hour and forty-five minutes to think through my options. There was no way I was going to go to pretrial and allow them to re-arrest me. What was I to do?

I informed my attorney that he needed to take my lease, the one I had with Robbie, and present it to the judge. Although I charged no rent, it clearly showed I had a tenant, and perhaps that would explain the alcohol in the house. I waited for a response from him and got none.

The following day, a Thursday, my daughter and four-year-old grandson came by for a visit. It was the first time since Ahlab had begun her assault on me that we could actually breathe and enjoy a day together. As I sat under the covered patio, charging my ankle monitor, my grandson enjoyed the pool with his mother. The day was idyllic. I watched as dragonflies dipped their wings in the pool, one after another. Their vivid colors of blues and greens entranced me, and I felt a peaceful calm. The Texas sun was perfect, birds were abundant, Hillary had chosen just the right music, the wonderful Jamaican sounds of Matisyu, and I couldn't have asked for a better day.

Then, the world came crashing in. Out of the corner of my eye, I caught sight of a police officer in a bulletproof vest with numerous weapons, scaling the privacy fence, then another over the back fence. My daughter acted quickly, grabbing her son and moving towards the back door. She gave me one desperate look and said, "Hide." We entered the home and moved to the master bedroom and bath area, thinking that it was a safe area. It was not; the police had scaled the fence and looked right through the windows of my bathroom window. At one point, Hillary went out and spoke with them. They informed her she could "stay and watch." What a sick thing to say to a daughter about the possible arrest of her mother!

Hillary made her way to my bedroom, keeping her son close to her body, with a deep look of fear in her eyes, and hugged me, telling me she loved me and that the home was surrounded. She needed to get her son to safety. She said she would go through the garage, which was the only safe way to exit, and told me to lock the garage door behind her. I did as she asked. After she left, I found myself in a standoff with the police. Hillary called and informed me that the *cul de sac* on which I lived was filled with police cars and that every street surrounding mine was lined with squad cars. There was no escape. Not that I thought of escaping.

I had committed no crime. What did they want? As I surveyed my bedroom and bathroom, I found myself face-to-face with officers. There they were, in my backyard, looking through my bathroom window; I was standing in my bathroom in a barely-there swimsuit; I said to him, please leave me alone; I'm having health issues, and you are on private property.

I called my doctor, I could feel a seizure coming on, I had taken my full dose of medication, they must have thought I was crazy when I explained the current situation and inquired as to whether I could take a second dose. What have I been reduced to? I felt very much like the mouse that had been trapped by a pack of cats and was being toyed with, day after day, week after week, month after month. When would they stop this obscene game?

I have no window treatments on my bedroom or master bath windows, so I crawled on my belly to the front closet and grabbed a hammer and nails. Thankfully, I found a few sheets in one of my drawers and nailed them up over the windows in my bedroom and bathroom. I stayed in that bedroom and placed enough food for Angel and myself for three days. Three long days. Dianne, Venomara, and even my friend, Michael, all begged me to give myself up. I refused. I would not surrender. I offered them this. They can burn the house down. I will not come out. They can drag me out. They have done that plenty of times before, or they can kill me. I had committed no crime; I was being persecuted and harassed for no reason, and I would stand my ground.

Hillary spoke with the police by phone, they told her they would give me three days, at which point they would break the front door down and taser me. She pleaded with them, explaining that I had seizure disorder and that a taser was dangerous. Her pleas fell on deaf ears.

Sunday afternoon, I noticed a police helicopter flying low overhead the house as I lay in the pool. Shit, was I just being paranoid? Or was this really happening? What a waste of the taxpayer's money. By Sunday night, I was experiencing rolling grand-mal seizures. I knew I needed help. I asked Hillary to get me an Uber to Sid Peterson Hospital in Kerrville. None arrived. Time crept by. I was edging dangerously close to a health crisis, and I didn't dare call 911. Look where that had gotten me before? I knew I needed help. I didn't give up. I finally found help.

I found a retired military member and a driver who also did bodyguard work were perfect! Brandon arrived at my home, and we enjoyed a long night together in the emergency room in Kerrville. They ran blood work, and sure enough, my levels were high for seizures. I was kept overnight and placed on I.V. lactic acid treatment due to my seizure activity. Upon dismissal, the doctors were very firm. I needed to be seen by a doctor within twenty-four hours, and I needed to remain on all three of my seizure medications twice a day as directed. I had no intention of not following his instructions; in fact, the first phone call I made upon arriving home was to Dr. Martinez's office in Boerne, and I made an appointment for the following day. I sent all of the paperwork from the hospital to pretrial to gain permission to attend this appointment.

I was pleased when Officer Moreno quickly responded with an email opening a "window" in which I could travel to my doctor's visit. In fact, she was overly pleasant. Physically unable to drive, I hired a driver. Something inside of me must have known. There must have been a sense, for as I left the house, I gave my housekeeper an extra large hug. It would be the last time I saw her.

I greeted my Lyft driver. As we exited the drive, I noticed a truck pull out in front of us and asked if he had noticed that truck there when he arrived? We made small talk, and as we turned the corner, we were surrounded by, I would guess, sixteen, perhaps eighteen, marked and unmarked Boerne and Kendall County squad cars. Several officers, all in bulletproof vests, again carrying plenty of heat, approached the car, calling out my name. I exited the car. You would have thought I was a big-time drug dealer or one of America's most wanted. My poor Lyft driver, his eyes were as wide as saucers. I'm sure I'll never get another lift driver to drive me! I was handcuffed, placed in a squad car and taken to the Kendall County Jail. There, I was booked on three warrants. I never made it to my doctor's appointment, regardless of my sharing the documents from the emergency room doctor and the emergent need to see my doctor.

After being processed, and of course, I knew all the guards by this point, I mentioned to them that all my medications were in my purse and that I had also brought the instructions with me from the doctors at Sid Peterson Hospital if they could kindly share this with Nurse Mac. I was then placed in the cold holding cell, where I would remain for the next two days. I was not given any of my medications during this time. I could only hope that once I met with the magistrate and was booked, they would give me my seizure meds and the meds for the blood clots in my brain. This medication is also vitally important. I also had been given orders for a MRI of the tumor in the pituitary gland in my brain, I was months overdue for this test, this was also denied me. I was about to get a rude awakening, medical care was far from my reach.

I wasn't surprised when I had my hearing with the magistrate when, once again, I was being booked on a "no bond." I waited a few more hours and was finally placed back in a pod. I was overjoyed when I entered pod A to find Emi there. Poor Emi, she was still there. She should have never been in jail, yet she was still there, a victim of the system. I also knew a few of the other girls. There were a couple of new girls. Two of them were lovers, which did not bother me. They were amusing and always good for a laugh. Both had spent their fair share of days in the pen. We got along well until they stole from me, and then I stood up to them. I told one of the girls to "take the first punch." She didn't, and then she threatened Emi that I would not tolerate it. I stood between her and Emi. At that point, the guards rushed in, and I was told to pack my things. I was moved to pod B. The guards were protecting me. I am thankful for that. My friend, Tink Nathan, a Colonel with the Texas Rangers and a world-renowned bow hunter, had been having conversations with the head of the jail, and I was in good hands. I enjoyed the peace and quiet of pod B. Then, as luck would have it, we had someone disruptive transfer into pod B, so they transferred me out of pod B and back into pod A.

Life in the pod was well; I had to make the best of it. I knew my family and friends were distraught. I had to keep telling myself, this could not last forever, even if it seems like forever. I was doing all I could, communicating with my attorney, and conducting myself as a compliant inmate. Each day I awoke, looking at the metal bunk above, I'd ponder, thinking who had laid there before me? What thoughts did they have? How long did they stay in that cell, were they missed, and what crimes must they have committed? Did they leave this cell, only to live in another?

During this time, I found out that my dear friend, Venomara, had larynx cancer. My strong, daring advocate was gone. Venomara and I had been friends for many years; I stood by her side when her ex-husband, an attorney, abused cocaine, dated strippers and destroyed their marriage. Venomara was devastated. He's a good man who fell hard into addiction, and he needed help; during that time, I visited with him during his stay at a nearby treatment facility. I would have done anything to help. Venomara's ex-husband was Ned. The attorney that would eventually betray me. I don't know to this day if Ned was duped into this whole mess by Ahlab or if he willingly took part. Ahlab has a way of engaging others into her schemes. I, at one point, offered to forgive him, but he declined and continued to represent Ahlab; I guess I got my answer.

Venomara had a son with Ned; that was her one bond with him, and although she knew of the wrongs he had done to me, she was torn out of the loyalty due to him through the ties connecting her through her son. This was complex. I was her friend in jail and was abused at the hands of her ex-husband, and she knew it. I would call her several times to see how she was doing. I am no stranger to cancer. I lost my mother, sister, and my husband to this enemy, and I do not fear this black devil. I also made frequent calls to Jeannie, the mother of Amanda Younkin Franklin.

Amanda crossed over on the burn unit at B.A.M.C. in 2011. Amanda was a wing walker, a pilot, and an inspiration to all who met her, and I promised her I would always look after her mother. She may have been in an induced coma. However, hearing is the last sense to go, and I know that Amanda heard my promises. I made good on those promises. For years, I sent checks to her mother and made regular phone calls to her.

Right: Amanda Younkin Franklin.

Jeannie was a constant source of support during those long days. I also founded a fund in her daughter's name to carry on her legacy. Jeannie had also lost her husband, Bobbie Younkin, in an airshow crash also. She is no stranger to pain and suffering. She is so dear to me.

I also spoke with my hunting buddy, Michael; all he talks about is hunting and fishing, which drives me crazy! Yet, that is what intrigues me about him. I'm a down-to-earth hunting and fishing girl. He is a treasure; he never stopped praying for me. He spent many a day out on the lake with Chief, a Cherokee Indian, praying for my release. When Ahlab stole my identity all those months ago, he saw right through her charade on Facebook. He knew something was up. I also spoke with my daughter, Hillary. What she went through, I will never imagine. There were days that she could not take my calls; it was simply too much for her, and I understand. I am so proud of the woman she has become, the mother she is, and the soul she embodies.

Things were becoming extremely difficult for her. She was dealing with the father of her child, to say nothing of raising that child on her own, finishing her degree, and with her mother in jail, it was becoming too much. My friend, Dianne, a D.A.R. member from Maryland, whom I had met when I accepted the Distinguished Citizen Medal from the D.A.R. back in 2018, was always available by phone. She kept in close contact with Jeannie and Michael. They kept a vigil. They never ceased in their efforts to secure my release. Calls to my attorneys, prayers, and calls to the jail were frequent. I could not have survived this ordeal without their constant and loving support. On any given day, life isn't as serious as the mind makes it out to be.

I was torn; do I remain in jail, fight for my rights? I was set for a jury trial back in May, then it was put off until July, then again reset for October. Now, I had no idea when I'd go to trial. This could go on for years. We had one sitting judge in the county, and she was dealing with a heavy caseload. She had already announced that my case was going to a jury trial. I had total confidence in this judge. I felt she was not only fair, she was sharp. I had total trust that she would see through to the facts of this case. I'd be standing on my first, second, and fourth constitutional rights. I also felt that the bodycam video would be revealed in court, and once the judge viewed it, the truth would be revealed. This could turn out to be one long, dragged-out mess. I also knew that with my standing as a public figure, the media would grab hold of this trial. That could be good, and it could be bad. I'd probably remain in jail until the trial. I'd be facing more attorneys' fees. I'd be unable to return home and see to business, unable to see my family. My heart ached to see my grandson and my daughter. My options were simple. I had only two. Plea, or wait for a trial. I tucked the thought away.

During my time back in the slammer, one of my fellow inmates, Keye, mentioned my former attorney, Stephen, and what an excellent job he had done for her. It gave me pause for thought. I had spent thousands of dollars on my new attorneys, but where had it gotten me? They were in possession of the bodycam video and had done nothing with it. I got the distinct impression, they were preparing for a big jury trial, they were in this for the gusto, so to speak. I had arrest warrants, three to be exact, and they had done nothing to protect me. But how was I going to re-hire Stephen when I still owed him money? I had just paid my importer for Karma, and the money in the bank was earmarked for the edits in the book. Ahlab had cleaned me out financially. I was still recovering from that. What was I to do? I had to find a way. I had to find some way, somehow.

I spoke with Hillary and devised a plan. I would give up Karma. I need to get back a portion of what I paid to my importer, empty both bank accounts, and use my annuity funds. With this combination, I could re-hire Stephen. The plan was in place. But would Stephen accept me? I called Tink and asked if he'd talk to Stephen. He agreed. Between Tink's call and Hillary rearranging my assets, Stephen agreed, and the deal was set.

Hillary dropped the paperwork off at the jail for me to sign, my importer needed the documents releasing the sale of Karma. A guard took me to the front, as I signed the document, it was all I could do to not cry, I was taken back to the pod and I did something, that for me, was unusual, I crawled into my bunk, pulling the blanket tightly up over my head and I cried, for hours. I felt the loss, as if I had lost another dog, how many more could I possibly lose?

My first meeting with Stephen was via the kiosk in my pod, just days before my pretrial date of September 18th. I was hopeful. All that hope was soon to disappear.

On September 18th, I was placed in shackles around my ankles, a chain around my waist that attached to the handcuffs; I shuffled my way to the awaiting squad car. I was lucky that on this day, Emi was also on the docket, as was another woman, Dora, a kind and lovely woman from another pod. We spent nearly four hours in a small holding cell as the court proceeded. Attorneys came and went. Stephen, my attorney came, and I was overjoyed to see him. We met in an adjoining room. He had a few brief questions for me. He also mentioned that due to having taken on my case once again only recently, he did not have a bond hearing prepared for me. He said he would call me later. Later never came. I was escorted back to the holding cell. Hours crept by when, eventually, our jailer told us we were to be taken back to the jail. We stood and were taken down the elevator, through the hall, by car, and back to the jail. As we pulled through the large doors, another squad car quickly pulled in next to us. The officer driving yelled out, "The judge wants Belt back." It was all very confusing not only for me but also for the guards and officers on duty. No one knew what to do. My fellow inmates and I were escorted to a holding cell that is typically held for the mentally insane. A creepy place, for sure, with one cement bench and a drain in the middle to pee and do whatever in...God!

We were eventfully led back to our pods. I later spoke with friends who were in the courtroom and heard what went on there. I heard that the judge yelled at my attorney, stating that this was her courtroom! It was all very confusing. In the end, I must have complete faith in my attorney. Stephen knows what he is doing and is acting on my behalf. He kept me out of that courtroom for a good reason and for my own good. In that, I must have faith.

Back in pod A, things were very pleasant. I was approaching a month in jail, this time, and knew the next docket would put me at a month and a half. That was my reality. As heart wrenching as it was, I was a part of the 'system". I met with Stephen in person. We agreed I would take a plea, something I had denounced doing in the past. Tink's gun was found in my car, and although it had his fingerprints on it and it was registered in his name, the facts are that it was in my possession. I would need to take the hit on that.

I would also need to be responsible for talking rudely to the 911 operator on the night of January 9th when I refused to go to the University Hospital. Which I did. I flatly did not want E.M.S. taking me to that butcher tank of a hospital, and I made that clear to the operator. Perhaps I overstepped my bounds. It's easy to do when you're having rolling seizures, and you're scared to death. I had already been taken by Boerne E.M.S. once to the wrong hospital on October 4th, 2022. I was not about to allow them to take me again. I have no memory of the conversations, and tapes of those calls were never played for me. Regardless, that's going to cost me dearly. *Shit!*

Stephen and I agreed a plea was the only way for me to get back. Before I met with him, one of my fellow inmates, Halley, looked me square in the eyes and asked me, "What would Randy want you to do?' I had to ponder that question. After a few moments, I looked at her, tears in my eyes, and responded, "He'd want me to be a Mimi and a Mama, he'd want me to get back to the business of helping people, he'd want me to go home, and that's what Randy would want." So, that is what I chose. I chose to plead my case.

Stephen told me it would take one to two weeks to work things out. He said one thing, one thing that would stick in my mind and would haunt me for months, a word of warning and of caution. He said, "Get out of dodge." I knew what he meant. I was no longer safe in Boerne. My home, with all that had happened there, held so many frightening memories of terror, fear filled me, each night I spent in that home. I also knew that selling my home in current market conditions meant taking a loss. I didn't care, I'd take any loss to be safe and free from those that might harm me or my family.

I had never intended to remain in that home; it was simply a short-term investment that went south due to the interference of others. Now, I'd need to gather my belongings and move back to the Bandera. I loved the place that Randy and I called home. I decided to take my attorney's advice, but first, I needed to get my affairs in order. There was much to do.

Two weeks came and went. I spent my time meditating. I repeated my prayer, my constant prayer, to those that have come before me, Blood of my Blood. My grandmother Iris, Aunt Rhonda, mother Celia, sister Audra, friend Vicki, friend Howard, husband Randy, and leader Amanda. Blood of My Blood.

Blood of my Blood!

Above left – Aunt Ronda LaVon, aged 15.

Right: My mother, Celia.

Above: Randy, my love – at his best. Below: Grandmother Iris VanBibber

At the two-week point, I was speaking with my daughter; we were both feeling quite helpless. We had no idea what was going on. Would I be released? Or was I facing time in a penitentiary? I said these words to Hillary, "When we have nothing left, we have to believe, just Believe."

Two weeks and two days later, a guard came to the pod and called out my name: "Belt, get ready."

I pulled myself together; I was not told where I was going; I could only hope it was to court, and what would be awaiting me at court was anyone's guess.

As I exited the pod, my cellmates called out to me, "Good luck."

I turned to them and said, "Luck will have nothing to do with it."

I was going to court, and the guard confirmed this. I was once again shackled about the legs and waist, handcuffed, and placed in a squad car. The weight of the chains seemed heavier this time, as if to remind me of the numerous times before. I had just spent the last ten months in jail, in chains. Much of that time in an isolation cell. I had no idea who or what was awaiting me. Has a deal been stuck? I was alone. My guard, Anthony, was a kind man, he had escorted me on several occasions in the past, I always felt a peaceful calm in his care. This was a Friday, the thirteenth of October, 2023, to be exact.

I was alone in the holding cell when Robert Arellano, Stephen's associate, came to speak with me. He did a thorough job of explaining to me that a plea deal had been struck and asked if I was in agreement. He did an excellent job representing my best interests in every regard. The thought did occur to me to ask to review the evidence, I was too afraid to do so, I simply wanted it all to end. I did ask if I would be allowed to see the bodycam video, he said yes, in his office. I felt I could not have asked for better legal representation. He explained to me that he had discussed it all with Stephen and the prosecutor in the case. I was impressed by his thoroughness and the way he presented all the documents. I could not have been in better hands. For these were the only hands I had.

One odd thing, that was added to my probation requirements, was that I have no contact with Trish and Tubbs. I of course, agreed, I wanted nothing to do with these criminals. I knew full well that these two individuals had been involved in the theft of my property and that Trish had been complicit in having me illegally put away in a mental hospital. Why, where are they now being listed on my probation requirements? The truth to this matter would come to light months later.

After signing both documents, I signed with the notary, and then I waited to be presented to the judge. Waiting in that small cell, the weight of the chains on my waist and my ankles, the cold of the steel bench on my buttocks, it's all an eerie and surreal experience. What contract had I been sent to this earth with? What brought me to such depths? My life has been filled with such highs and such lows, learning experiences, for sure.

I have a great deal of respect for the judge in my case. She is the first woman to sit on that bench. She won that seat, in a male dominated county, of which I have great respect. She has a great presence. A warmth about her, yet she can be quite stern. She is obviously intelligent, yet thoughtful. She takes her role seriously. There is no doubt in my mind that she looked my case over thoroughly and was fair and just in my sentencing. I'm sure her docket was full, yet, she took the time to hear mine and of that I am grateful.

I entered the courtroom, my shackles rattling, announcing my entry as I shuffled my way into the courtroom. I must have been a sight, dressed in my striped jailhouse black and white uniform, the "costume," as I called it. I was asked to stand at the blue line and face the judge. She looked down at me with kindness and empathy, and as she explained to me, I was giving up my right to a jury trial and access to all witnesses. She also made me aware that my offenses carried a penalty of up to ten years in the Texas Department of Corrections. This was serious, and I needed to treat it as such. I had broken the law. I was guilty, and I pleaded guilty. I had agreed to take a plea.

I accepted six years' probation for each offense, and each would run concurrently. I left the courtroom, and as I entered the anteroom, Mario, the probation officer assigned to me, greeted me and handed me his card with my upcoming appointment. I knew I'd be required to wear an ankle monitor for three months to track my movements, and having that placed on me might take a week, so I was resigned to wait another week in jail. I was elated when Mario informed me that I'd be going home that very day, that day! Tears fell down my face in torrents. I reached for his hands and held them in mine. He doesn't know me. All I could say was, "May the Gods bless you."

Back at the slammer in my pod, it was glorious to share the news with my cellmates. I was most excited because I'd be able to give them my food, clothing, colored pencils, and all I had recently purchased from the commissary. Many of them did not have funds for commissary items and were cold in the frigid room. Most were facing hard time in the pen. I always felt blessed to have the ability to purchase goods from the weekly commissary and I made a point of sharing. Susan had stage four breast cancer. I wanted to make sure she was kept warm, so I gave her numerous items of clothing. Emi, who had recently been granted release to an assisted living facility and would be leaving soon, I had some special gifts for her.

We always watched *Yellowstone* together on Sunday nights. I would make her cheese dip with Fritos, so I made sure she had that. I gave Halley a pantry full of food and clothing, she was just recently sentenced to seven years in the pen and I wanted her to enjoy her last days in jail, it was good to spoil her a bit. Marsha, who suffered from psychotic episodes, many times stating that she'd kill people... something we had learned to live with; well, I gave her many things, including eight sets of colored pencils. I hope coloring calms her down. The day I left, I had attached to the top of my bunk a printout of a Native American lore of the two wolves. As it goes, which wolf will you choose to be today... the world of the humble, loving, caring, good wolf or the aggressive, eager, starving, greedy, bad wolf... It's the wolf you FEED...

Then, finally, my name was called over the intercom. It was time. It would be a long fifteen minutes before the guard appeared to escort me through the several sets of locked doors. Each of my cellmates hugged me and offered their goodbyes, I gave them my last words of encouragement and love. I gathered the few belongings I was to take home and those I was obligated to turn in. My sheet, mattress, blanket, cup, and spork. I paused at the doorway, taking in the cell, and those within, offering a parting word, as I exited the door, I turned to them and shouted, "Kacham Cie..." I love you, in Polish.

The guards led me out and handed me the clothing I had booked in those months ago, by now, wrinkled and disheveled. I didn't care. I was on cloud nine. I was going home. I entered the small room, the same room I had dressed in my uniform so many times before when I was booked into custody. On this day, I was dressing to go home. I gleefully put on my shoes and three-inch heels and remained there, tapping my heels and whistling a tune I was in no hurry to go. I just wanted to hum a song and tap. I wanted to feel the texture of my own clothing on my skin, the height of my heels, and the closeness of freedom. I was nearly there. The guards must have heard me. They called out, "Belt!" Then, the door opened. We proceeded out to the desk and poured over my personal effects, my jewelry, my books, and my prescriptions.

I slowly put each ring on each finger. Every diamond on every ring, sweet memories of the past, all were in order. I wore Randy's wedding ring, as well as mine, among an assortment of other rings. Each had a meaning, a place in time, a memory, cherished. The guards made a few jokes about my frequent stays, and my response was, as always, a humorous one: "I need a frequent flier program."

I knew that I'd be coming home to many messes once again. All my funds had gone towards attorney's fees. I had given up my new pup, Karma, which was gut-wrenching. My daughter had also informed me that Ahlab had changed my will, making herself the sole beneficiary. Why does she wait till I'm in jail to remember to tell me these things? I would need to have a new will drafted as soon as I got out of jail. What legal document did that woman not forge? First, my P.O.A., perhaps the deed to my home, social media information, custody of my animal, computer access, banking info? The home and property had also been put to good use and were also trashed. Now this? I would once again be dependent on food bank food.

I had two books about to be re-published and one new book to come out. I had money owed me I needed to collect, my car was about to be towed, my auto insurance had been canceled while I was in the slammer, proceeds from the sales of my first two books were mysteriously going to a bank account that we could not track. God knows what else. What a mess. None of this matters; all of this is fixable. What matters is I'm home, I can cook, I can clean, I can sit by the fire pit, I can lay in the pool, listen to the birds, and snuggle with my cat. I can plant flowers, and I can have a cigar. Best of all, I could spend time with my family. Damn, life is good! Life is different, it has its shadows, it's cast with new walls, that I must walk around, but damn, it is mine and it is good!

My father called me. He had remained in close contact with Hillary during my stay in jail. He knew the strength I possessed and had complete confidence in me that I'd make it through this trial in my life, just as I had so many other obstacles before. His first words to me were, "Happy to hear your home." Then he went on to say, "You're like a bird, a jailbird, that is, you keep flying in and out of jail. I found that amusing.

I then rang my daughter. I got a bit of bad news. Due to the fact I am now a convicted felon, I can no longer be around my grandson, at least temporarily, she is currently in a custody suit and until that is settled, I must be patient. I must be humble and understand, this comes with the territory. It is painful, gut wrenching. How many layers of pain must they bring me, they cannot break me, and I will not allow them the slightest splinter. This experience I must pass through, live through and suffer beyond. My reach is greater than theirs. This is my new life; I am a convicted felon. Collateral damage is tough to swallow.

Once home, I was back to relying on food bank meals, a humbling experience, indeed! My car insurance had been canceled in my absence; the car payments had not been paid. Hillary had also brought to my attention that Ahlab had drafted a will giving her all my assets upon my death, and my five hundred thousand life insurance policy had also been laying outside of the safe. She may have placed herself on that as a beneficiary. I needed to address all these issues. I had the first two books ready for re-publishing, and this one is nearly ready to publish. My plate was full, to say the least. Yet, freedom never felt so good. I had faith that it would all work out. I would somehow find a way to, one by one, address each issue and cross each item off my list.

I began the task of getting my home back in order, as I opened the door to the garage and viewed the contents, knowing I needed to store the car there until I could get caught up on the payments, I went to work, stacking boxes to one side, preparing enough space to park the car. Once I had enough space, I literally shoved the car in, I did however, damage the car in the process, damn! Through my resourceful nature, I was able to catch up on the payments, reinstate the insurance and begin the process of putting this shattered life back in order. Jesus! How many times would I have to go through this process?

During all of this, I never gave up, and neither did my friends, quietly looking for Risqué. For many reasons, there are things that cannot be shared in this book. The search for Risqué went on for over a year and involved hundreds of people and law enforcement. I will forever be in their debt.

A few of the first things I did, once home, was oil my saddle and boots, load them up in the car and take a long drive in the Texas hill country to the J L Bar ranch and spend a day on a horse with my friend John, a Texas Ranger. We had been speaking for several months about riding together. It was food for my soul, riding in the hills, surrounded by nothing but the landscape I love, enjoying catching up on life and world events with John. We were accompanied by John's dogs and his pet deer and were ever watchful of rattlesnakes. The gentle rhythm of the horse, my body in the seat of my saddle, I felt as if I was eating for the first time in months. I also spoke with Ted, my importer, and ordered a new pup, Karma, who would arrive soon, and I would know the sweet embrace of my new pup once again. All would be well, and I knew it. They may have taken much from me in the past year, but they can't take away my dignity. I had a mountain to climb, I knew it, but, I'd climb it, I'd win this battle, I'd fight, and I'd win.

This entire sick and twisted tale, this long and languid story, all began and consisted of the greed of one solitary person, Ahlab. Why, when I had loved her so much, had she grown to hate and despise me and to turn others against me. The police worked off information gained from her, and the hospitals did so also. She planted the seed all those months ago that I had been having psychotic episodes when, in fact, I suffered from seizure disorder. A well-diagnosed and medicated condition. The police were simply operating off her misinformation. I had guns in my possession because I lived in a place of fear. She had raided my home, stolen my beloved dog, attempted to take control of my person, threatened my family members, and stolen my identity. I lived in constant fear. So, I resorted to carrying weapons. This, in the end, carried a heavy penalty for me.

Let this be a lesson to all that one person, one trusted and loved human being, can destroy your life. Or, in my case, nearly destroyed it. How I survived her reign of terror is beyond reason. My friends and family ask, "How did you?" They are amazed that I am still alive. The only answer I have for them is that it was my constant belief and prayer to those who came before me and those who are to come. My spirit guides. They kept me safe. I will never give up hope of finding Risqué. I met with the vet who last saw her. Ahlab had taken her there on November 7, 2022. Using my credit card, she had Risqué vaccinated and acquired a year's worth of supplies. She also secured an interstate travel document for Risqué. She produced a false document, drawn up by Ned, the attorney, in which it states she would be taking over my estate and my person.

Chilling, isn't it? The vet shared that Ahlab stated she would be traveling with the dog. With this information, we renewed our efforts to look for Risqué and turned our sights on Ahlab. We will never give up and never give in. If Risqué is alive, she is due for her shots; the one year is approaching, and she has a tattoo and a chip. We have D.A.R. members, military members, law enforcement, friends, and German Shepherd owners across this great nation, all looking. She will, and must, one day come home.

I received a call from my friend, Venomara, she stated that she needed to stop by and drop off some documents that were given to her by her ex-husband, Ned. I could not for the life of me, think of anything, that I had previously provided Ned that would have been in his possession. When Venomara arrived, she laid a large stack of folders on the table and asked that I sign a release for them. The release was on Ned's letterhead. I carefully looked over the files and was shocked to see that years of my medical records, my EEG reports, and personal notes from my neurologist, Dr. Mehendele, were all laying before me.

Why on earth had Ned had access to these private documents? Then it hit me, they had been kept in my safe, and Ahlab had helped herself to the contents of that safe. My mind was reeling. These medical files had been kept from the mental hospitals, the jail and most importantly the police and the judge in my trial. Ned and Ahlab had portrayed me as a woman with a mental instability when in fact I had a diagnosed brain injury, with EEG reports, a long file of medical history to back this up by one of this nation's top neurologists. The damage they have caused me is unspeakable.

I was also heartsick to hear that the threatening phone calls to Dr.V. continued. Ned and Ahlab continued their threatening phone calls, in an effort to dissuade her from protecting me. Phone calls that were many times recorded. Ned would lose track of what he was saying and would slur his speech, many times calling on Sundays and at odd hours. She would not budge, she stood on the side of the truth. She made every attempt to help me during my time in the mental hospitals. Dr. V. was my doctor and therefore should have been granted access to see me; Ahlab barred her visits to me, that is breaking the law, a Federal offense. My doctor is an amazing and strong woman, I feel so distraught that she has been drawn into this tawdry situation. This situation has also been handed over to my insurance company to investigate.

Ahlab was so loved by me. I was supporting her financially. However, she got greedy. She was not working. She had custody of my niece, which she has now lost to the State of Illinois. Her son is now in custody or soon should be for the rape of my niece.

My children have suffered at her hands, as have my animals. My niece, my beloved Trynn, may be the biggest victim in all of this. I pray she isn't. I know that my mother and my sister have a say and some pull that they are watching and waiting from the heavens. Ahlab will not have the last stand. Justice may not be swift, yet I have faith that it is yet to come. The Gods will pour fire.

I learned so much in this past year, so many lessons. I met so many wonderful people. A few people I'd just as soon forget, but more I'd like to remember. I heard their stories about life, love, and tragedy. Some I'll keep in my heart forever. Their stories will be like Mandalay's. Colors that light my world and give me hope and caress my days with color and my nights with light. You know who you are. I needn't mention you by name.

La Fin

I thought I was done; it was over, and the nightmare was complete. I was moving on. Putting back the pieces of this broken life. I had one asset left, the one thing Ahlab was unable to obtain, which was my home. She came close; she had a realtor lined up to sell my home, and she had the P.O.A., an estate company, lined up to sell what valuables she had not already taken. She came damn close. The realtor refused to sell the home because the deed was in my name alone. By the grace of the Gods, I prevailed.

So, here I was. I decided I'd refinance the house. I needed cash to pay my debts and regain my life. I needed some cushion. That plan didn't work. I simply didn't have the income with interest rates so high to qualify for the loan. I'd have to move on to plan B. At one point, my daughter suggested I file bankruptcy, and simply purge myself of the losses dealt my way from the situation with Ahlab, I flatly refused. I was my mother's daughter, and she would never hear of such a thing.

My daughter also wanted me to be a "Mimi and a mama," to lay in the pool and collect my checks, to live a quiet life, but that's not me. I had a story to tell. I made a promise to those I had met in the mental facilities, those who cried out in the dark rooms. Their cries would not go unheard. I was placed on this earth for a purpose. Yes, my purpose was for burn survivors and those suffering the effects of traumatic brain injuries; for so long now, that purpose may be for more voices to be heard. I may need to speak at fire stations and share with those first responders just how special they are to the lives they save. I have a purpose, and it is not to sit at home and lead a comfortable life. I could feel and sense that purpose expanding to include the experience of what I had just endured over the past year. A voice was calling me. The voices of many, the voices of the unheard. I knew in my heart that I would need to listen, not only to write their stories but also to share their stories in public speaking venues. They would not, or could not stand for their own rights, I needed to stand. I simply had to. Just as I had to all those years ago for burn survivors, I had to stand. So, I choose to stand. As the lighthouse on the rock weathers the storm, so must I.

I also got word that Risqué, my female German Shepherd, may be alive and well. I never gave up hope, I never gave up, and I never gave in. I decided to put some "heat" on Ahlab in Illinois, knowing she was under investigation for the rape of my niece. In conversations with Round Lake, Illinois police, it was shared that Ahlab was "no stranger" to local police. What better time for her to break and spill the beans. She was sure to throw others under the bus, so to speak, and disclose the location of my beloved dog. D.A.R. members across the country had been working for a year; they never gave up on their efforts to find my Risqué.

With their guidance, all done in the quietest of ways, we constructed a plan. The plan worked. We in no way set out to entrap her, we simply waited for her to entrap herself. Within days, Ahlab was sending Facebook messages to D.A.R. members across the nation. Most included misspelled words; one, she sent to a D.A.R. member, we all had a good laugh at, she stated, "LOVE FAT". We all found this amusing, as she's a very large woman. She obviously meant to say she lived "too far." She was grasping at straws. She would send numerous messages to D.A.R. members, then immediately block them so that they could not respond. A cowardly act, for sure. She was definitely feeling the heat. Her messages were shared with authorities.

Meanwhile, I had numerous other issues to attend to. One of the conditions of my probation was that I wear an ankle monitor to track my movements, I would no longer be on horse arrest. However, I would need to pay the tracking company five hundred and fifty dollars to have the device attached. With just dollars to my name, I was scrambling. I sold furniture, was eating food acquired from the food bank, was attempting to refinance the home, going through drawers attempting to find any old cash

Left: My rock, my daughter, She never left my side during these dark days.

I'd stashed, Ahlab may have overlooked in her looting of the home.

My probation officer rang me on a Friday to inform me that I had just days to come up with the funds to cover the costs and to have the monitor attached. I did just so, just in time. I am blessed with very kind care and very good and fair officers who truly want the very best for me. Probation is not a bad thing. It is much like having my mother back with me, being home by midnight, not drinking, and not doing drugs. Be the best version of yourself. Simple. Did I deserve this? Perhaps. I had a gun in my possession, yes. I was afraid. I had my home looted, my identity stolen, my dog taken, and my daughter and my grandson threatened. I was terrified. I had a gun. I had no bullets. I was afraid of that gun, but I had it, nonetheless. Ahlab had brought about a reign of terror. My life and that of my family had been ripped to shreds by the greed of this one hateful person.

My probation included a six-year concurrent sentence for the calls to 911. I have no memory of those calls, nor was I ever given a chance to hear those calls. Another point I might make is that I was afraid and fearful that E.M.S. might once again take me back to University Hospital in San Antonio. A place that terrified me in the past. I wanted to go to Sid Peterson in Kerrville, I was told that I spoke rudely and with poorly chosen words to the 911 operator. This was during my call to 911 in which I called for help during a seizure episode, I remember nothing. For this, I will remain on probation. By the letter of the law, I am guilty.

I remain patient in regards to the return of my beloved dog, Risqué', Lya, in Washington, a D.A.R. member, U.S. Military Veteran and owner of a service dog is laying the groundwork to pick up Risqué. Darlene, D.A.R. member in Seattle, is working with Lya. D.A.R. members across the country are all quietly working. Police in four states are all quietly working. I wait. It is Monday, October 30, 2023.

As the week progressed, Ahlab was questioned by Round Lake Heights Police; she was dishonest with law enforcement, stating she had no idea as to the whereabouts of Risqué, when in fact, just the day before, she had messaged a D.A.R. member stating she knew the location of the dog. This information was shared, and I was asked to provide more information to officers in Washington, Illinois, and Texas. I did so and let the chips fall where they may. I found solace in the one thing I had left, my sanctuary. I meditated. When your home is not your sanctuary, all you have left is your mind and the universe. I enjoyed the company of close friends and family.

Vengeance is not mine. Karma may come, or it may wait. All I know is that I must make my own way through this new life of mine. This fractured and somewhat frail life I've been left with. I must look at it with new eyes and find joy in each of the blessings I have, and I have many. I have a lovely home, friends who will go to the mat for me, a daughter who never left my side, and a cat named Angel. The birds sing to me each morning, with songs of renewal and hope, the Texas sun kisses my lips, and I watch the sunrise through a window, not in a jail cell. I am free. Libertad. I am grateful, I am humbled, and I am extraordinarily blessed. I have lessons, they are mine, tough ones at that, I can cross them off my list, my earth lessons. How many will I be given on this contact? Only the stars hold this information.

Life was becoming quite complex, with authorities in three states awaiting word to reopen the case of my stolen dog and the theft of my property. Boerne police were stalling. Why? When we clearly had a paper trail of evidence. We had attempted to reopen these cases on numerous occasions. State Farm was equally frustrated as they had also made attempts to subjugate the case regarding my stolen property. Yet, Boerne P.D. buried it. What or whom were they protecting? A part of me wanted to wash my hands of the entire thing; another part wanted the truth, the whole truth. I certainly had enough on my plate.

Three books in the works, with a fourth in my head, a new pup about to ship, and my health, my fragile health that had taken a beating this past year in need of repair. Do I walk from all of it? Do I give up on Risqué? Do I let them win? Do I hope she is well cared for and happy? My mind was reeling. I was poking a big dog; of this, I knew certain. Was I putting myself at risk? Was it worth the risk? Or should I simply move on, give up, and give in?

In the midst of all this, on Veterans Day, I was enjoying coffee at Black Rifle coffee shop when I met a man, Kyle Stanbro. Not many people have the last name Stanbro. I asked if he might be related to Kodey Stanbro, my former bodyguard, and wouldn't you know, Kyle was his father. Nothing in this life is by coincidence. Nothing. I spent a bit of time chatting with him, and shared just how special his son was to me, that Kodey had come into my life and offered me some comfort during a very discomforting time. I hope he took that message back to Kodey.

Life was becoming complex. Much was happening. My mind went back to the words my attorney Stephen had said to me while I was in jail: "Get out of dodge." I decided he was right. I no longer felt safe in Boerne. Each time I glanced at the front door, memories would flood my mind, I would re envision, the police bursting through the door, of them grabbing me, my body flailing about, in the throes of a seizure and them throwing me into handcuffs, tightly behind my back, then dragging me through my home. It was all I could do to keep myself composed, living in that house of horrors. I would need to sell the home. I knew I'd take a hit on it with current market conditions. That really didn't matter. My safety and the safety of my animals and my family came first. I needed to get to higher ground, so to speak. So, I did just that.

I was also knee-deep in final edits with Dorrance Publishing for the release of the re-publishing of *Remarkably Intact* and *Silent Warrior*. Both books will soon be available in full-color hardcover with additional photos. We were behind schedule. The first two edits contained numerous errors. This was frustrating. Dorrance is a top-notch publisher. I would find that my editor had left the company, and much of my edits had been lost in the process. My new editor was simply attempting to pick up the pieces. The original plan to publish all three books, which included *My ValHalla*, had been changed. *Remarkably, Intact* and *Silent Warrior* would proceed with a publication date before Christmas. *My ValHalla* would be put off for a spring publishing date. This wasn't necessarily bad news as I found myself still in the heat of things and adding to *My ValHalla*. We are unsure of whom, but someone is currently acquiring all the revenues from my first two books that are currently in circulation. In the past, I had always donated all proceeds to the Moonlight Fund. So, I needed to get the first two re-published and get those revenues firmly directed into my accounts. I had faith. It would take patience. It would take time. I would soon have an income. Numerous libraries across the country, friends, and followers are anxiously waiting to purchase the books once they are published with Dorrance. I have a large following, many are also anxious for the release of this book and for the story to be revealed. The day was coming. I simply needed to wait. That's one thing you learn, sitting in jail, is patience. Hours upon hours of sitting, waiting, looking at walls, the bunk above yours, a seven by ten cell, a room with no windows, you learn that all you have left, is pure patience.

The search for Risqué was heating up across the nation. In Illinois, Ahlab had been questioned by Round Lake Heights police. During questioning, she provided the police the location of my dog, stating it was with the veterinarian. We can only assume by this that she meant the vet she took her to back in November of 2022. Yet, she had also, in writing, stated to a D.A.R. member that the dog was with Trish in Olympia, Washington, and in yet another, more cryptic message, and once again, misspelled message, she offered that the dog was being held at Trish's mother's home in Sierra Vista, Arizona. What were we to believe? Ahlab was a thief. She had looted my home, attempted to sell my home, stolen my identity, my dog, and so much more. Were we to believe anything this greedy, lowlife individual said? Well, that's all we had. She was throwing her co-conspirators under the bus, so to speak. D.A.R. members and police were all working in each state. However, when we contacted Boerne police, offering them more documents, a list of witnesses, contacts in various states, ownership documents, and much more, they disregarded the case. What or whom were they protecting? The vet? The thief? Or was it something much more sinister? Had they for so long, disregarded the evidence, closed cases, protected the thieves, that they had boxed themselves into a corner that they felt they had no way out of? The police brutality report from December had been closed; the report of the theft of the dog had been closed as well as the theft of the items from my home had been closed. Why had all these cases been closed? Each and everyone was not investigated, completely disregarded.

I so wanted all this to end. It had been more than a year of this. I was on probation for two offenses. They had their pound of flesh. Leave me alone! I had a lunch date with Dr. V. planned. I was looking forward to that. As we spoke on the phone, she mentioned that she had, in the past two weeks, received three disturbing phone calls. Ahlab had called her out of the blue from a number Dr. V. did not recognize. She left a message stating that Dr. V. needed to "be on her side." Dr. V. found this amusing. On the side of a thief, a liar, a woman who attempted to bribe her with stolen goods and money she stole from Celia? A woman that abused animals?

She went on to say that a day later, she received a second call, this one from the attorney, Ned. In his message, he called her a "f...ing bitch," and went on to say he was going to have her deported. Now, mind you, he's leaving a message on the phone of one of the most well-respected trauma surgeons in San Antonio. A woman who holds two PhDs and medical licenses in two countries is the widow of a world-renowned surgeon and has been a U.S. citizen since 1974. He made a second call to her, which was also recorded; he was equally as threatening. It was obvious that Ahlab and Ned were running scared. Something had happened. I knew these were both desperate people, and they had stooped to desperate measures in the past. I needed to be careful and wait for the shit show to begin. All I wanted was to move away, get out of Boerne, and begin my new life. I wanted out, away from all this. They can have their own drama.

November progressed, and with it, the one-year anniversary of Risqué's theft. A difficult day, indeed.

I sat by the pool, gazing into the waters, that wasn't enough. Then I dove into the deep end, remaining there for some time. Fourteen feet down, where there is no sound, no one to hurt me, no memories to invade my mind, no chains around my ankles or waist. Just the water, the pure water that surrounded my body, buoyed by spirit and my mind in those minutes. I allowed my soul a bit of tranquility, of peace and void of all memories.

I opened my safe. Evidence, more than a year's worth, compiled by myself, my private investigators, and police in four states, came tumbling out at my feet. It was daunting. I truly did not even want to look at it. It brought back so many memories. So much suffering, so much loss. But I had to. So, I sorted through it all. I had been quite careful. I made sure that not only did my P.I. have copies of a significant amount of this evidence, but I also made sure that third parties had copies of all with specific directions as to what to do should something happen to me. It occurred to me, on more than one occasion, that there were those that probably would like me out of the picture. However, the picture does not go away. The colors do not fade, they remain for all to see.

I made a file for Ahlab and each of her co-conspirators. As you can imagine, Ahlab's file was quite large, filled with document after document of each and every incident. As I pondered sharing that file with my attorneys, the fact that that evidence could put her in jail, I knew that I had not the slightest intention of doing so. I did, however, want to recover my dog, Risqué. Just how to do that and not put Ahlab behind bars might be tricky, as she was the thief in this case, as was Trish.

Vengeance is not mine. I would leave this up to the Gods, for it is not mine to decide. Karma comes to us all. For me, it would come in the form of a fur ball flown in from the Czech Republic; for Ahlab, well, that was to be determined. Her Karma may take more time.

I spent my day attempting to pull together a meal out of what I had left of the food given to me by the Hill Country Bread Ministry. They had been donating food to me since I was released from jail, and I was eternally grateful. I had learned a few skills in jail, such as how to make a meal with ingredients I'd purchased through the commissary, mix them with ingredients provided at meal times, and voile! I did the same with the items provided to me by the food bank. On this particular day, I made chili out of some curious ingredient, but chili nonetheless. Then, there was a tap at the door. A kindly gentleman introduced himself as Daniel and said he was there to drop off a Thanksgiving meal from Hill Country. You can imagine my glee. I'd have turkey with all the trimmings! I was over the moon. He asked if he might back his truck into my drive, which I found curious. It must be one big turkey, I thought. Then, it began, load after load of groceries. Canned goods, fresh carrots, and potatoes are fresh from the ground. Chips, cookies, tea, and orange juice, I could go on and on, and yes, there was a thirteen-pound turkey with all the trimmings! After he made his last load in, he asked if there was anything else he could do for me. I kindly asked him to pray with me. I asked that we pray for guidance, that soon I would be selling my home, and that I needed guidance for this new journey. We held hands and did just that. I was grateful for his visit and sent him on his way.

He left, and I set about the task of putting it all away. It felt so good to have groceries in the house. I turned the chili on the stove down to a simmer and rearranged the refrigerator, throwing out the old food store I had been saving for a "rainy day". I sent a text to my son... "Thanksgiving dinner, at Mom's place, 4 p.m. Let your sister know."

Above: Back where I belong, near the still waters.

For years, I was the one caring for people through my nonprofit efforts. I was the one filling the refrigerators, paying the medical bills, furnishing the homes, and hosting the retreats. Counseling those I cared for on the mass of pills that had been prescribed to them, which included narcotic pain medications, something I stood firmly against. I will admit it was awkward to receive help. Yet, I had to, and I am grateful. I am humbled, and I don't quite have the words to say thank you, because thank you is not enough.

Thanksgiving Day arrived, and what a glorious, sun-filled Texas day it was! I woke early, wanting every detail of the day to be just perfect for my son, his wife, my daughter, and my grandson. I spent hours laboring over the stuffing, preparing the turkey and side dishes, and I even You-Tubed how to use my microwave convection oven for the sides. I inspected the home one last time to ensure it was just so-so. I took great pride in knowing my grandson would be delighted when he saw the recent additions I had made to his art room. Every detail was thought out. Jarred arrived first. He found me outside, relaxing with Angel, my cat, by the pool. She loved being outside, exploring every nook, flowerpot, and boulder was hers to explore. We fell into easy conversation. He commented on my hair. I had worn it down, this day, the first time since cutting it off, all those months ago. His wife Vanessa was ill on this day, so it was just the two of us playing catch up after several months of separation. I inquired about his business', his wife, small talk, did my best to avoid speaking of jail, mental hospital and all talk Ahlab. Hillary and my grandson arrived nearly two hours later. I expected the warm hug of my grandson and the caring eyes of my daughter. There was no hug, no I love you Mimi, or HI Mom, just distance. What I got was something quite different. Rather than running to me with his usual hug, my grandson had to be encouraged and cajoled into hugging me. My daughter kept a watchful distance from me. I was confused and dismayed. Yet, I said nothing.

I went along with this, preparing the meal, showing my grandson his art room, and making small talk. My grandson appeared frightened and unusually uncomfortable and I saw the look of real fear in his eyes. We snapped a few photos, thumbed through my Santa photos of years past, and reminisced about how much Jarred had grown since those early Santa photos. It would be days before I understood why I received such a chilly reception and the true nature of my grandson's fears. I had truly blocked events of the past out of my mind. Such was the day, only months ago, when my grandson and my daughter spent that carefree day at my home, in my pool.

As I sat on the porch, charging my ankle monitor, police officers, clad in bulletproof vests and carrying numerous firearms, converged on my property. That day was etched into the memory of my four-year-old grandson's mind and my daughter's mind. My home was no longer a safe, loving environment. It had become a house of horrors. I needed to leave this place for them and for me. I needed to build new memories and find a safe place where my grandson could feel safe, where he could once again hug me, and where I could live without the threat of invasion. The terror they struck into the hearts of my family was not necessary. I fear the damage caused will last a lifetime. My daughter continues to live with the trauma caused by events this past seventeen months of horror. I wish there were some way I could erase it from her memory, but there is no way, I can only pray, that time, and a future of good, loving experiences replaces that of the past.

As I spent my days preparing the home for the real estate photographers, I listed the house with Fore Premier Properties in Kerrville, Texas. My time was also spent on preparations for the arrival of my pup, Karma. Christmas was also fast approaching. So much to do! My mind wandered back to thoughts and memories of founding the Moonlight Fund. Why did I co-found that beautiful organization that helped tens of thousands of people? In truth, it was born out of my own suffering, my burn injury, and the abuse I suffered as a child. It took me nearly thirty years to fully realize that my injury had a true purpose on this earth, a destiny much bigger than myself. How can a person sit at the bedside and look into the eyes of a burn patient and, with such empathy and understanding, listen to their story? How can a person hold a grieving family member who has just lost their loved one to a burn injury and feel the shudder of their body and feel sobs so deeply? Only if you have felt it yourself. My accident was no accident; it was all meant to be. So, if I was burned, beaten, and raped as a child and used that for the good of others, what, I ask, am I to do with this situation?

I can only hope that it does not take me thirty years to realize, as did the Moonlight Fund. The message I take forth from this tragedy in my life will need to help others. It must, or it was for nothing. My suffering, all the pain, was for nothing. The collateral damage spent. What is the message of not trusting those closest to you? Perhaps. To take better care of your health, you bet. Keep all that you love, your precious family, pets, and friends close by your side, and show them all the love that you have. Never stop telling them, never stop delivering that message to them, never stop. To remain true to your promises, even when the fog is thick, and you can't seem to see, believe in your promises because they are yours. However, be careful of whom you offer those promises to.

We all enter this world with a contract, and mine must have been vast and certainly complex. Burned, beaten, and raped at an early age. Then, I survived a traumatic brain injury that I should not have survived, yet I did. Now, this is when so much came against me. Life is a paradox. Everything is dynamic energy, and the most abundant of these is unconditional love.

As I made preparations for Thanksgiving, I couldn't help but think that last Thanksgiving, I was in a mental hospital. Imprisoned illegally, but imprisoned nonetheless. I did my best on that day to cheer up my fellow detainees. Faith, a beautiful African girl, and I had struck up a friendship. I remember the first time I laid eyes on faith. I was still in the other unit. We entered the dining hall, and there she was. This stunning, tall, young African queen. Hair to her waist, in braids that took me back to my days in Africa. She sat alone, yet every eye in that room was on her, every ear peeled to her every word. She was magnetic. She was a spirit-filled being, of this I knew to be true. She saw and felt things that were otherworldly. She was incredibly intelligent and loved by her mother, a mother who brought her to the U.S. from Nigeria as a child for a chance at a better life. She struggled with depression. I could not help but feel love for that girl. As dinner time was approaching, we found our way in line among the other "crazies"—there was always plenty of entertainment in that place. We walked the long hallway silently. I'm sure each of us was having the same thoughts, wondering what our families back home were doing on that day. Were they missing us as they sat down at the table? We took our place in line, just as we did for every meal. I greeted the cooks and servers, cracking jokes and making pleasantries.

On this day, the music played loudly, and I couldn't resist it. I broke free of the line and found my way back to the dishwashing station. A small, private area near the staff. There, the music was even louder, and I danced. I danced, and I danced. I was free. I was still a captive; there were still bars on the windows and guards at the doors, cameras on every wall, and plenty of staff on duty, yet, at that moment, I was free. I lost myself in the music, and in that moment, the bars on the windows melted, liquid gliding to the floor, like a stream to the rivers beyond.

This Thanksgiving would be much different. My son Jarred, his wife Vanessa, my daughter Hillary, and her son, my beloved grandson, would be here with me. Can I begin to share the deep love I have for each of them? I know the pain they must have suffered over the past year. Today, we would begin on a path of healing. We would be together. We would break bread, laugh, paint, and treasure memories that were long forgotten. Food for this tortured soul of mine. Yesterday, on a trip to Bandera, I stopped at my favorite bakery and picked up a cherry pie. I wanted the meal to be just perfect. I added an additional set of chalk and markers to my grandson's art room; he had yet to see the new easel I had only recently added to the room, and I was eager to share it with him. I had hoped that Karma, my new pup, would have been here, but alas, the breeder had not shipped him from Prague yet. I'd have a few days to wait for his arrival. Just as well, we didn't need that diversion. My attention needed to be solely on my children and my grandson on this glorious day. It would be a day full of confusion for us, yet, it was also full of hope, because I believe that we all knew that I would soon be selling that place and that this time next year, we'd be celebrating

Thanksgiving in my new home, free of all the frightening memories associated with this place. Free.

There exists one last piece of business I would need to address, both for my health and my peace of mind. Since January, several of my attorneys and my private investigator had been denied requests to view or receive a copy of the bodycam video of my January 9 arrest. During the early morning hours of that day, I called 911 three times. I was having grand mal seizures. I was told I would be taken to University Hospital. I flatly refused and went on a tirade, saying things I probably should not have said to the operator. I was terrified of returning to that place. I continued to beg them to take me to the Kerrville Hospital.

On the third and final call, I finally gave in and said, "Come, please, I need help." Minutes later, two Kendall County deputies arrived at my door, burst into my home, and placed me in handcuffs behind my back. They dragged me into my living room and watched as I had several seizures in handcuffs. E.M.S. did finally arrive; they took my blood pressure, which was through the roof high, yet, even as I begged them to loosen the cuffs, they allowed me to seize cuffs. They left me there, in the custody of the deputies. This is a memory that terrifies me to this day. My attorneys, my private investigator, and I have been unable to gain access to the bodycam video. Both the Boerne Police Department and the Texas Attorney General's office denied their requests. They and I received numerous letters stating act upon act as to why they would not release the footage. I guess they thought they were attempting to create a mare's nest and hoped we'd simply give up. We didn't. It's important to note that at the time we were asking, the sitting Attorney General, Ken Paxton, was being impeached by Texas Governor Greg Abbott.

Yet, even when that dust had settled, we continued to make requests that were denied. This went on for months. The letters kept coming, and our requests continued to be denied. My private investigator decided to use the Freedom of Information Act to secure the footage, which also fell on deaf ears, and he was denied the footage. Finally, after nine long months, the second attorney I had hired to represent me was given access to the video. I asked to see it. Unfortunately, I was arrested and sent back to jail the next day. It was at this point that I decided to rehire Stephen to represent me. He was my first attorney in this case. He was also able to gain access to the video.

During our jailhouse meeting, when we discussed my accepting a plea, I brought up the video. He asked what I was going to do with it. I pondered his question and answered honestly, "I don't know." I knew in my heart that I had forgiven those officers. Had I forgiven the E.M.S. workers? I'm not so sure about that issue. They were trained medical professionals. How could they leave a woman with a documented seizure disorder in handcuffs, experiencing rolling seizures that were causing damage to her handcuffed hands? This is something I struggle with to this day. Stephen's partner, Robert, also mentioned the video, stating that if I wanted to view it, I had forty-five days from the time of my release to come by their office and do so. I struggle with this. Do I really want to see this? Do I want to relive that event? I'm already suffering from P.T.S.D. due to this event. My health has been damaged, and I'm well aware of that. I find myself becoming paranoid of the police of Boerne, watching each step I make. Even the sight of a police vehicle brings about much stress. These are behaviors of someone who has experienced severe trauma. I've been trained to assist those who have experienced such trauma, and here I was, in the heat of it myself.

This experience, combined with the December assault and all Ahlab had done, was testing my mettle. It would take all my strength, my fortitude, and my life-learned lessons on survival to get through this. Forgiving those that had hurt me would not be enough. I recognized that I'd have to heal myself. I needed real help to mend this shattered soul of mine. Taking steps to remove myself from any possible future harm was only part of the solution. I'd need real help. I asked my therapist to connect me with a trauma counselor. I could not change the pain of the past. What I could do was work on me. The repair job was mine to do.

One thing the judge ordered at my sentencing was mandatory counseling. I am unaware if she understood that I would be undergoing trauma counseling for the damage caused by the brutality of local police, as well as the harm done by my cousin. Regardless, I am eternally grateful for this added benefit to my probation. I began my counseling immediately with Wendy at Kendall County Mental Health. She was incredible, I felt an immediate trust and bond with her, after a few sessions I began to share things with her and she recommended I begin trauma counseling with Herlinda in her office. I had been trained to deal with patients returning from war, those dealing with P.T.S.D., and knew all too well that I was now suffering and I was in need of help. I could not survive this alone. I needed help. Herlinda was a God send. As you can imagine, my walls were high, I did not have the highest trust level, it took a few sessions to truly begin the process, but once we developed a rapport, the results were remarkable. Her instruction, combined with my move out of Boerne, set me on a path to healing. Each week, I looked forward to our Skype calls, knowing that I could share my challenges and accomplishments from that week. I pray that everyone receives such sound support. For me it has been remarkable.

E'chapper

When dreams become reality, it's a good day, and mine has come true. I quickly received a cash offer on the Boerne home. I had just one week to pack and move. I found a home in the Texas Hill Country with some land, hired movers and set about the task of packing. Karma was young and the home I purchased was not yet finished. I informed the builder I'd live in a tent on the land, for, I was moving, leaving the nightmare behind. My builders were aware of my situation, and moved quickly to ready the home for me. As fate would have it, a furious storm arose on my moving day, I would not allow that to stand in my way, I was going, come hell or high water. The rain was so bad that my movers were unable to move many of my items onto the property, so we made the best of the situation. I was just damn happy to be away from Boerne and all the drama.

Once settled into my new place, I viewed the neighboring land and set about purchasing all within sight. I wanted land to roam, carefree walks with Karma, wildflowers to enjoy in the spring and wildlife in abundance. I built a patio, a fire pit and a large pond out of the remaining rock not used in the construction of the home. Backbreaking labor, for sure, yet, I loved this type of work, I'm no stranger to hard, physical labor and I took such pride in each project. I also purchased a Spanish Timbrado Canary, giving him an Arabic name, Sarani. The fourteen foot ceilings of my home were now filled with his expansive song. My nights were filled with the setting sun and colors that created a vivid landscape all their own, followed by an array of stars and always the moon, my constant companion, my guardian on this journey of mine.

Above: Rebuilding a life, nearly destroyed, I am HOME!

I also had my probation transferred to my new county. I had truly enjoyed my previous probation officer in Boerne and had the greatest hope that I'd find similar support in this new area. I was not disappointed. My new officer was extremely easy to talk to, in fact, I found myself sharing more of my story than I meant to share, perhaps due to her easy nature. I feel safe in my new home and surroundings. I continue to receive threats from Ahlab, via text, however, these texts are immediately shared with investigators and I can now simply shrug them off. I am free of her and her reign of terror. My attorneys have drafted numerous documents to protect my assets and my family from any future intrusions from this person. I am free. Libertad!!!!

Had I just experienced my own Greek tragedy? Yes. I was taken down to the murky depths of despair, in the waters deep. Beyond light, into darkness, I thought I'd never once again experience. I was afraid, fighting, and utterly alone. I climbed a mountain, the rocky shores of forgotten seas, to swim out. Navigating waves and currents, I didn't think possible to pass, and yet I did. Only to reach a shore filled with no help and no source of light. I found my way through pure grit and determination. My source was deep within me. It was me. I was that little girl that had survived so much. How could I not survive this? I looked to my left and to my right; no help presented itself. I would have to do this on my own. Seeking and searching, I began the journey. I fought, I gathered, I bartered, I won some and lost some. I was winning on days and losing on others. This would be a journey that only I could take.

Each of us has a journey; that journey is ours alone. How we navigate it is of our own choosing. The pitfalls, the barricades, and the blockades that impede us cannot stand in our way. We must choose to look at each with the eyes of a child. Those eyes see nothing but goodness. Clarity and inspiration, a soul that needs no explaining. A body that seeks no judgment. This is and will always be what I will strive for, the eyes and the wisdom of a child.

I survived, I fought, I won, and I lost, I endured. More than a year of the worst suffering of this life. I lost so much, yet; somehow, I gained more, so much more. I sought, and I found the wisdom and the comfort of... My ValHalla.

For more by the author, Celia LaVon Belt

Her two previous titles, the award-winning memoir *Remarkably Intact*, and *Silent Warrior* are available through Amazon! A portion of profits from sales of these titles and from speaking events will benefit burn survivors.

Made in the USA
Coppell, TX
01 November 2024

39207122R10138